Making Music

Making Music

Ann Sayre Wiseman and John Langstaff
Illustrations by Ann Sayre Wiseman

STOREY KIDS

The mission of Storey Publishing is to serve our customers by publishing practical information that encourages personal independence in harmony with the environment.

Edited by Deborah Burns
Art direction by Meredith Maker
Text design by John Bidwell and Melanie Jolicoeur
Cover illustration by Ann Sayre Wiseman
Text production by Melanie Jolicoeur

Printed in the Canada by Transcontinental Printing
10 9 8 7 6 5 4 3 2 1

Library of Congress Cataloging-in-Publication Data

Wiseman, Ann Sayre, 1926–
    Making music : how to create and play 70 homemade musical instruments / by Ann Sayre Wiseman and John Langstaff ; [illustrations by Ann Sayre Wiseman].
        p. cm.
    Includes index.
    Summary: Includes instructions for making and playing a variety of simple musical instruments from ordinary household items.
    ISBN 1-58017-513-9 (alk. paper) — ISBN 1-58017-512-0 (pbk.: alk. paper)
        1. Musical instruments—Construction—Juvenile literature. [1. Musical instruments—Construction.] I. Langstaff, John M. II. Title.

ML460.W529 2003
784.192'3—dc22
                                                                                    2003054218

Ideas, credits, and thanks to: The many people who invented, explored, and created musical instruments at The Boston Children's Museum when I was there, and the 1972–73 staff of the Advisory for Open Education in Cambridge, Massachusetts — especially Cornelia Voorhees.

The Education Development Center, and Dan Watt and Emily Romney of the Elementary Science Study who conceived the Musical Instruments Recipe Book and Whistles and Strings published by McGraw-Hill. Paul Earls, Mariagnese Knill-Cattaneo, and Suzanne Pearce for helpful suggestions. Carl von Mertens for instrument building help. Bonney Laurie Rega, Vanessa Kirsch, and Sarah Bartholomew for posing with instruments so I could draw them. Mills & Boon Ltd., for permission to reproduce the scale on page {56}, from *Making Musical Instruments* by Peter Williams. Albert Whitman & Company for the random pipes made from garden hose described on page {56}, adapted from *Music and Instruments for Children to Make* by John Hawkinson & Martha Faulhaber, copyright © 1969 by Albert Whitman & Co.

— A.S.W.

Sarah Cantor, David Coffin, Brian Holmes, Shaun Conroy, Tro Langstaff and Sarah Tenney are friends who came up with answers to my questions. — J.L.

CONTENTS

Projects listed below in red type = how to make instruments.
Projects in black type = how to make music with them.

Beginning Notes

From Ann Sayre Wiseman

Whenever I hear that music, art, and creativity are being cut from the school budget, that learning by doing is being eliminated from the curriculum, I write books to show that creativity is the best and most long-lasting way to learn about life, facts, truths, how things are made, and how things work.

Creativity does not require a special budget or special teachers; it requires imagination, common sense, and resourcefulness. Time to explore should be a basic part of all teaching and learning. When the hands can make something that works, the body is delighted, the mind is validated, and immediately you become a teacher yourself who can pass the skill on to someone else who wants to learn.

Making musical instruments is an important part of creative thinking, and nature has given us amazing sounds to work with. You can find rhythm and sound everywhere: the wind blowing through trees and whistling over holes, thunder in the sky, waves on the sand, rivers rushing by, rain drumming the roof. Singing, humming, slapping, clapping, tapping — wonderful sounds, a scale of notes, free of charge.

We have made instruments that copy these natural sounds. A gourd strung with a sinew or vine makes a crying sound. Anything can be used as a drum. Blowing through reeds makes different notes.

When I was working at the Boston Children's Museum I took a group of kids to the dump with a wooden spoon in each hand to collect good sounds. Car parts were the best. We then went to our kitchens and tapped pots, pans, everything we could hang

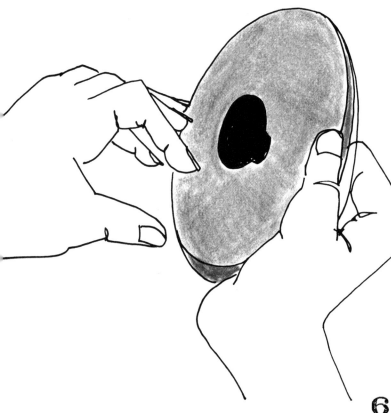

from strings. We blew into pipes and reeds. We collected sounds for our DAM GOOD DUMP BAND and you can too. Hang your sounds from a fence, a shelf, a rack, or the branches of a tree. Invite your friends to come and make music, compose a symphony, write a score.

John Langstaff will show you how to make music and rhythm, how to syncopate, how to work together in a group and make an orchestra, how to conduct, and how to write a score. John has been teaching for years and has written many books of songs and musical games. Here are his suggestions for making music with these instruments.

From John Langstaff

The little girl stood thinking, motionless, in the middle of the room, facing a semicircle of children holding improvised instruments, and contemplated how she might begin the music.

Looking over her attentive "orchestra," she slowly raised her arm and suddenly pointed to one player. The whirring,

metallic sound of an eggbeater began quietly, growing slightly in volume as the conductor's other hand beckoned pitched notes plucked at random from a kalimba — dozens of little notes shimmering over the low drone. Eventually she introduced a different texture, seeds in a large gourd shaken to a furious crescendo. Next she coolly pointed to a child clasping two large pot lids, which he clashed together as primitive cymbals. Now the young conductor fervently waved her arms, urging the players on and indicating the entrance of the remaining musicians.

At this point there was a density of sound in which I could hear a xylophone, notes of a recorder, and the pattern of a single drum making a continuous sound underneath it all. As the cacophony rose to a climax, the conductor held up one hand to signal the clanging, dominating pot lids to cease. Suddenly she held both hands above her head, focusing her players, and then her arms shot down, outstretched, to cut off the music abruptly.

The silence was stunning — but only for a moment. To my surprise, the young conductor-composer's hand flew out to cue in again the original first instruments. I heard the low growling drone of the eggbeater joined by the sparkling notes of

the kalimba, just the two quiet instruments continuing on and on . . . until she wiped them out with a pass of her hand to end the piece.

I was fascinated. Her music had ended as it had started. Here was a very young "composer" fashioning a score right on the spot, as she conducted her orchestra of homemade instruments for the first time — dealing with the same problems Beethoven had. How to begin? Where to go and how to get there? How to end?

This is the essence of making music together, and it can be experienced using homemade instruments, as described in this book. Children have a natural affinity to rhythm, and this book offers ways to get them immediately involved. As they become more and more engaged in improvising with their instruments, they learn about basic musical elements such as tempo, dynamics, phrasing, and polyrhythms. As they create their own compositions, they naturally learn how to shape them. Presented effectively, this music making is like a fascinating game to children — and to adults as well. Entire families can have musical fun together. Let's begin!

KITCHEN THINGS THAT RING

Look around the kitchen,
hang utensils from a string,
tap them with a pencil or a fork
to see if they ring.

Make a gong by hanging a metal tray
or a resonant garbage can lid. Strike it
with a soft mallet (see page 39).

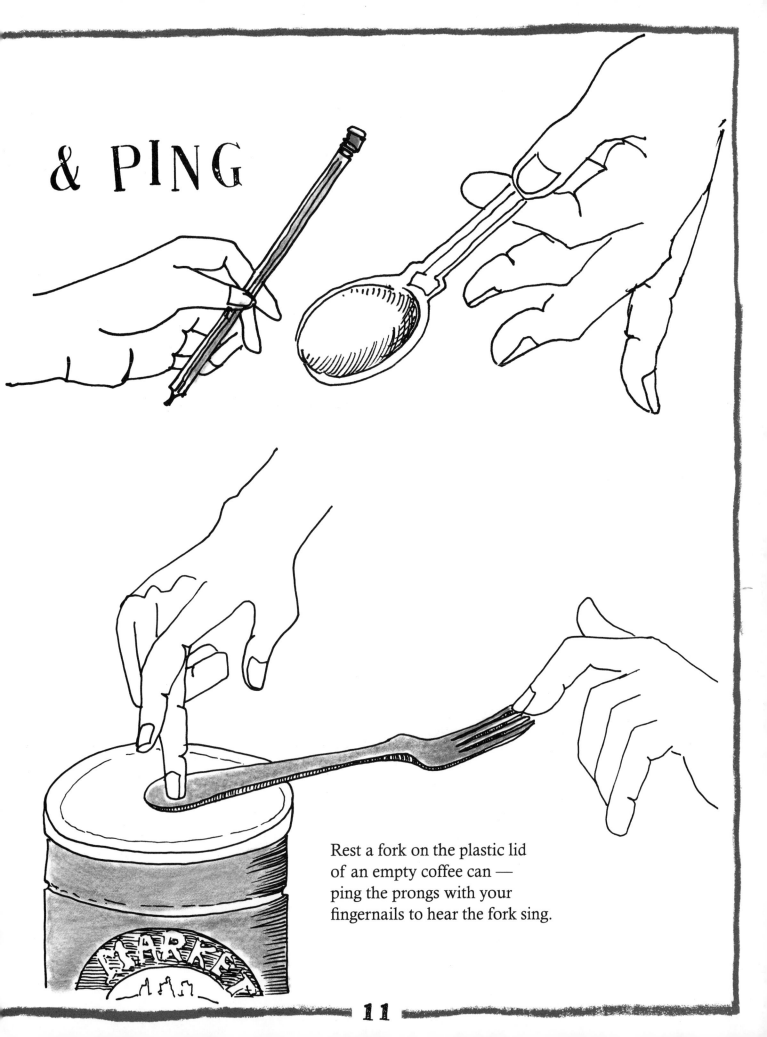

& PING

Rest a fork on the plastic lid
of an empty coffee can —
ping the prongs with your
fingernails to hear the fork sing.

SCRAPERS & RASPS

Look around the kitchen

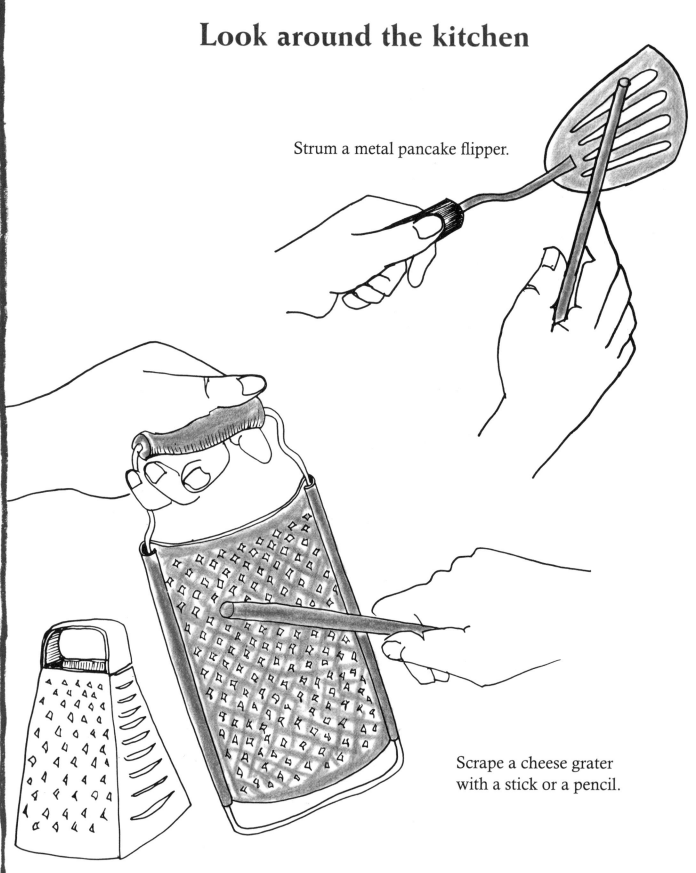

Strum a metal pancake flipper.

Scrape a cheese grater
with a stick or a pencil.

THE GUIRO
from Latin America

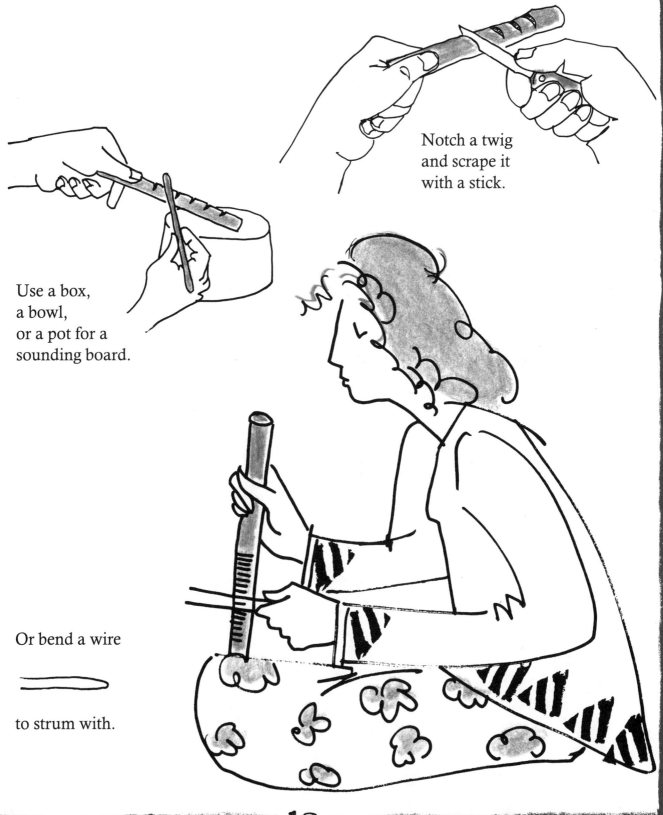

Notch a twig
and scrape it
with a stick.

Use a box,
a bowl,
or a pot for a
sounding board.

Or bend a wire

to strum with.

NAMES & NOTATION

Re-BEC-ca
TOM
E-li
MEL-a-nie
Pe-NE-lo-pe
AN-ne-ke
Hi-RO-ki
Jo-SE
Te-RE-sa
Eu-GENE
RA-chel
Al-ex-AN-der
E-LIZ-a-beth

Say your name all in one beat.
Have the group repeat it.
Go around the circle
with the group echoing each name.
Then repeat your own name
on one beat, over and over,
adding names around the circle.
Keep it going. Add clapping.
Listen as the rhythms pile up.
Now try it with percussion instruments.
Listen to the different patterns.
These are called "polyrhythms."

FRUIT SALAD

Four players each choose a different fruit. Say the name of the fruit in one beat. Then play that rhythm on your instrument.

This is a composition. All four players start together on the count of 1 and read across their line, saying or playing the fruit name. ✳ **means a beat of silence.**

Count →	1	2	3	4	1	2	3	4
Apple ♫	apple	✳	apple	✳	apple	✳	apple	✳
Pear ♩	✳	pear	✳	pear	✳	pear	✳	✳
Pineapple (triplet)	✳	✳	pineapple	✳	pineapple	✳	pineapple	✳
Plum ♩	✳	✳	✳	✳	✳	✳	✳	plum

Children's Street Chant

Here's a standard way to write, or "notate," music.

Say the words first, then play them on an instrument. This round can have two or more parts, each part entering as the previous part starts the second line.

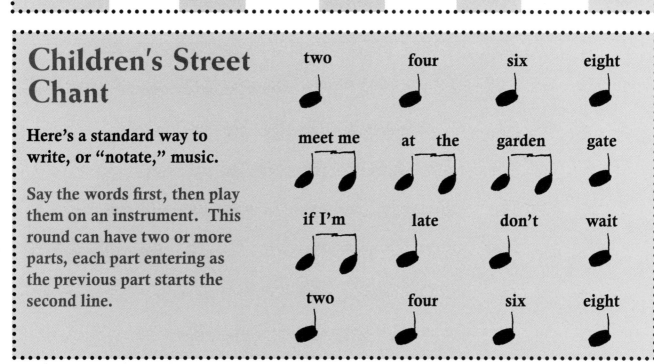

two four six eight
meet me at the garden gate
if I'm late don't wait
two four six eight

CRYING WATER BOWLS & COOKING POTS

Stainless-steel bowls with ½ cup of water
swirling around
when struck on the bottom
make strange sounds.

American composer Harry Partch built
an array of glass bowls, called "cloud
chamber bowls," and wrote several
pieces for them.

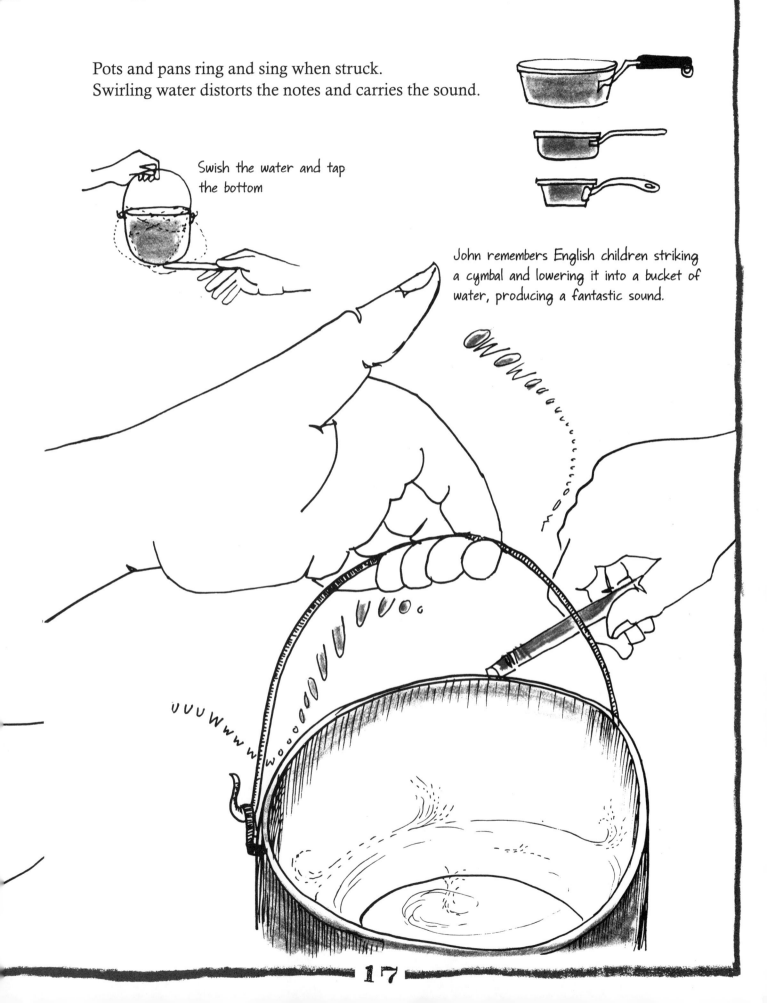

Pots and pans ring and sing when struck.
Swirling water distorts the notes and carries the sound.

Swish the water and tap the bottom

John remembers English children striking a cymbal and lowering it into a bucket of water, producing a fantastic sound.

17

POT COVER CYMBALS

Clash, ring, and ping

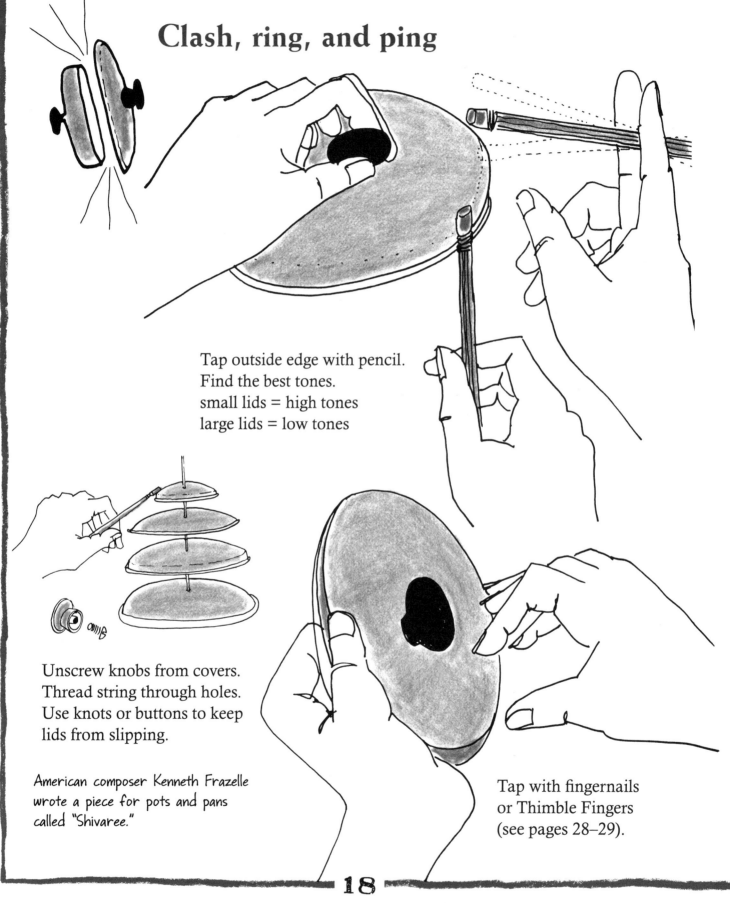

Tap outside edge with pencil.
Find the best tones.
small lids = high tones
large lids = low tones

Unscrew knobs from covers.
Thread string through holes.
Use knots or buttons to keep
lids from slipping.

American composer Kenneth Frazelle
wrote a piece for pots and pans
called "Shivaree."

Tap with fingernails
or Thimble Fingers
(see pages 28–29).

CLOCK MUSIC

Opus 1: A Little Piece for 2 Pot Covers

You will use two pot covers, a fork, the clock score, and a real clock with a second hand.

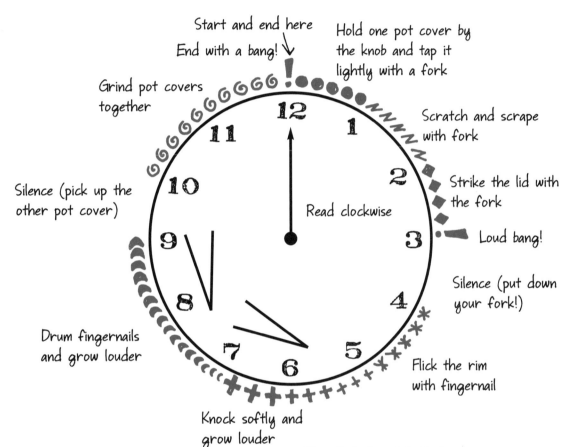

Start and end here
End with a bang!

Hold one pot cover by the knob and tap it lightly with a fork

Grind pot covers together

Scratch and scrape with fork

Silence (pick up the other pot cover)

Strike the lid with the fork

Read clockwise

Loud bang!

Silence (put down your fork!)

Drum fingernails and grow louder

Flick the rim with fingernail

Knock softly and grow louder

Here is a clock score for solo player
or several on a part.
The second hand of a real clock
will be your conductor.

Study the list of sounds at right.
Find on the clock score
when each sound is to be played.
Then grasp one pot cover by its knob.
Start at 12 and tap it lightly with a fork
for 5 seconds as shown.
Continue around, waiting for the cue
for each sound.
You will end back at 12 with a big bang!

Tap lightly with fork = ●●●
Scratch and scrape with fork = $\mathcal{NNN}$
Strike with fork = ◆◆◆
Loud bang with fork = !
Silence = (no symbol)
Flick pot rim with fingernail = ✳✳✳
Knock softly with knuckles = +++
Drum your fingernails = ❱❱❱
Silence = (no symbol)
Grind two pot covers slowly together = ❻❻❻
End with a bang! = !

A crescendo, indicated by ＜, is when you start softly and grow louder.
A diminuendo, indicated by ＞, is the opposite: you start loud and grow soft.

BELLS · CHIMES · TRIANGLES

Stemmed wineglasses,
rubbed with a wet finger
around the lip edge,
sing.

Water glasses filled
to diminishing levels,
tapped with a spoon,
give different tones.

Clay flower pots
hung from a rod
(try different sizes)
can be struck gently with a stick.
(A cracked pot won't ring.)

Bells sewn on a ribbon
can be worn on legs and arms.

A fork or nail will ping;
a bent steel bar, suspended,
can make the sound of a triangle.

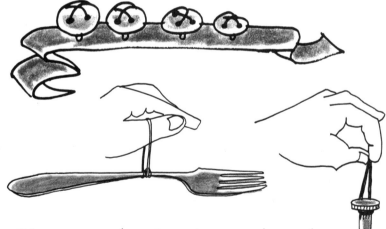

Take an unpainted metal coat hanger and a yard-
long piece of string. Wind the middle of the string
around the hanger hook. Wrap the ends of the
strings around your index fingers and then stick
your fingers in your ears. Lean forward so the
hanger swings freely enough to strike an object —
chair, table, etc. You will privately hear the most
amazing sound of big tolling bells. You can attach
more strings to the coat hanger so that several
people can hear the bells at the same time!

GLASS HARMONICA

You can make clear pitches
from thin-rimmed glasses of water
filled to different levels.
Wet one of your fingers.
Rub it around the glass rim.
Try playing a song.

Benjamin Franklin loved this sound
and built an instrument to make it
easier to play.
He called it the "Glass Armonica."
He composed his own pieces for it
and traveled through Europe playing it.
Foot pedals rotated a series of glass bowls
of graduated sizes set in a trough of water.
When a finger touched the moist, spinning bowl,
it produced a clear musical tone.

Mozart liked the sound of the glass harmonica
so much that he wrote several compositions for
it, and Beethoven wrote one, too.

TAMBOURINE

Head

To make a tambourine head,
stretch thin hide, rubber inner tubing,
canvas, or fabric over a hoop.
(After fabric is stretched over hoop,
saturate it with diluted white glue
to give head a better tone and tightness.)

Hoops

Hoops can be made
of cardboard, heavy belt leather,
or flexible plastic.

Try embroidery hoops.
(Stretch hide or chamois skin
over the smaller hoop and
secure with the larger hoop.)
Thread clappers or tie them on.

Clappers

Clappers can be made out of seashells,
screw eyes, buttons, washers,
coins with holes, or bottle caps
flattened with a hammer.
Drill or poke holes in the hoop.
Thread clappers or tie them on.

bottle caps

In each of the caps
tap a big loose hole.
Thread them on
a wire or a paper clip.

MARACAS: RATTLE & CLATTER

Use any empty container:
plastic, wood, paper,
glass, or cardboard,
filled with stones, rice, beans,
peas, or sand; or a natural gourd,
filled with its own dry seeds.
Make two: shake one in each hand.

Fill a small or large
milk carton with pebbles.

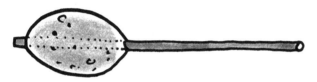

Fill a **plastic lemon** with seeds
and slide it on a chopstick.

Seeds inside a gourd will
rattle when dry.

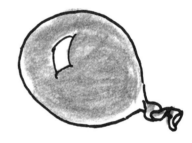

To make a **balloon shaker,**
insert four or five paper clips
before you blow the balloon up.

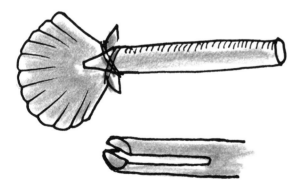

Scallop or clam shells can be clamped
together. Split a dowel tip to hold the shells.
Put tiny pebbles in the shells. Attach with a
strong elastic, string, or shoelace.

Two **paper soup bowls**
or **aluminum pie pans,**
glued together with pebbles
inside, rattle.

RAINSTICK

Sew wire through
a cardboard or plastic tube
to make a maze
for rice, dried peas,
or sand to run through.
(Instead of wire, poke nails
all the way into tube.)

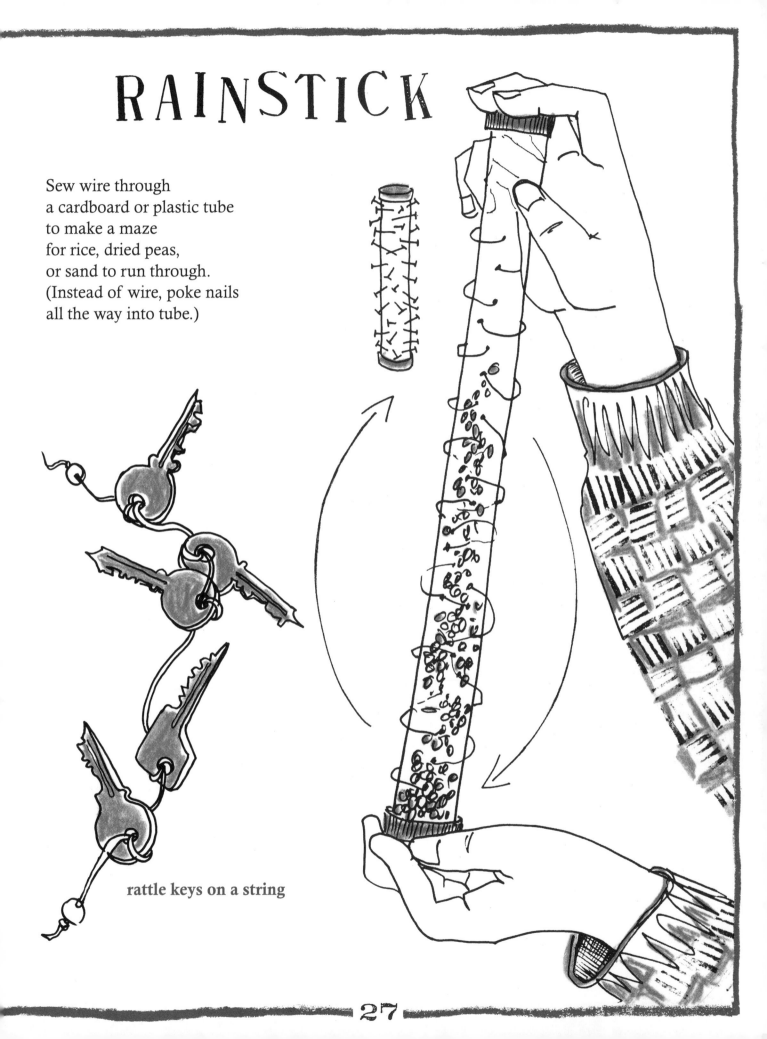

rattle keys on a string

THIMBLE FINGERS
& TAPPING GLOVES

Buy 10 thimbles that fit tight.
Metal or plastic is all right.
Tap on wood, tap on stone,
tap on metal, tap on bone.
Every surface has a sound.

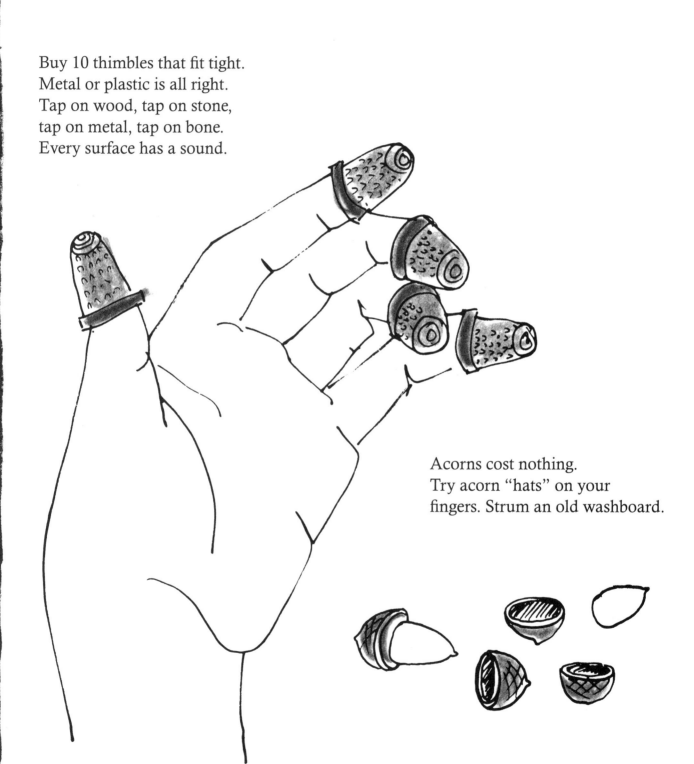

Acorns cost nothing.
Try acorn "hats" on your
fingers. Strum an old washboard.

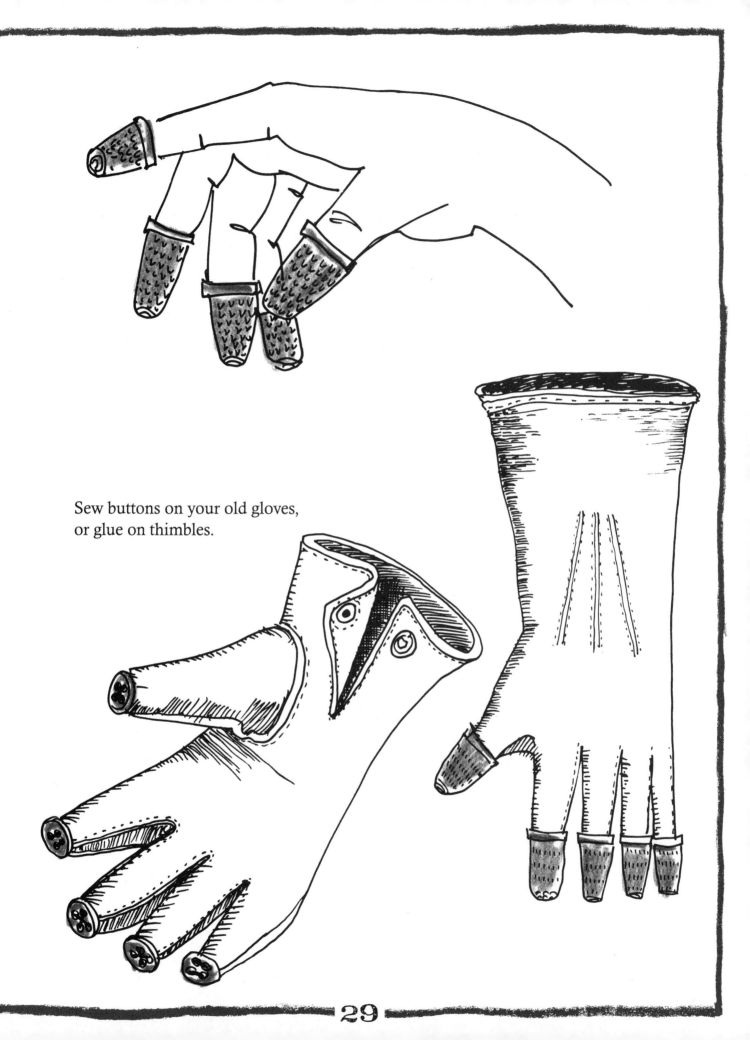

Sew buttons on your old gloves,
or glue on thimbles.

CLAVES & RHYTHM STICKS

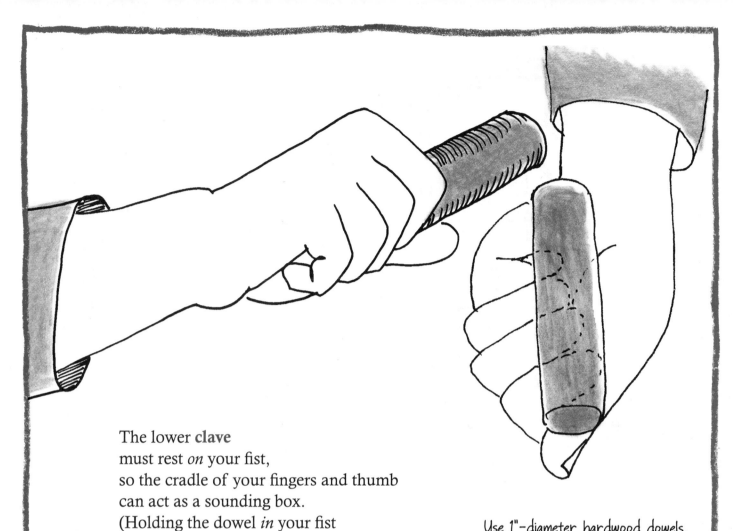

The lower **clave**
must rest *on* your fist,
so the cradle of your fingers and thumb
can act as a sounding box.
(Holding the dowel *in* your fist
will "deaden" the sound.)

Use 1"–diameter hardwood dowels,
4" or 5" long.

SAND BLOCKS

Tack sandpaper on wooden blocks.
Tack on tape or ribbon as hand-holds.
Scratch the blocks back and forth to play.

JINGLING JOHNNY

Shake
your
stick
or tap
it
on
the
ground.

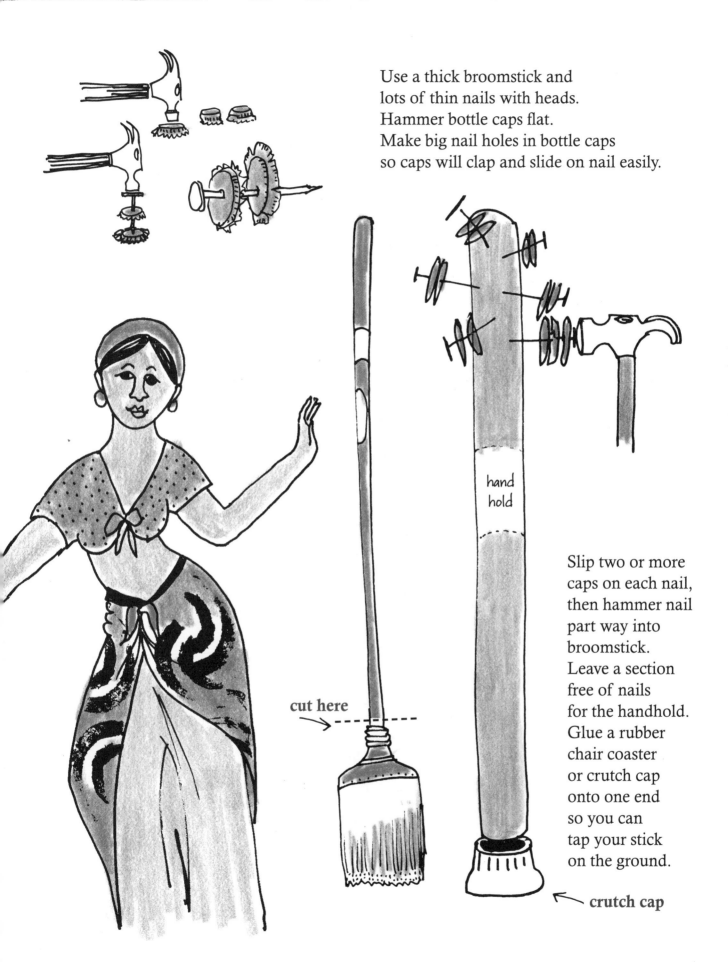

Use a thick broomstick and lots of thin nails with heads. Hammer bottle caps flat. Make big nail holes in bottle caps so caps will clap and slide on nail easily.

hand hold

cut here

Slip two or more caps on each nail, then hammer nail part way into broomstick. Leave a section free of nails for the handhold. Glue a rubber chair coaster or crutch cap onto one end so you can tap your stick on the ground.

← crutch cap

CASTANETS & CLAPPERS

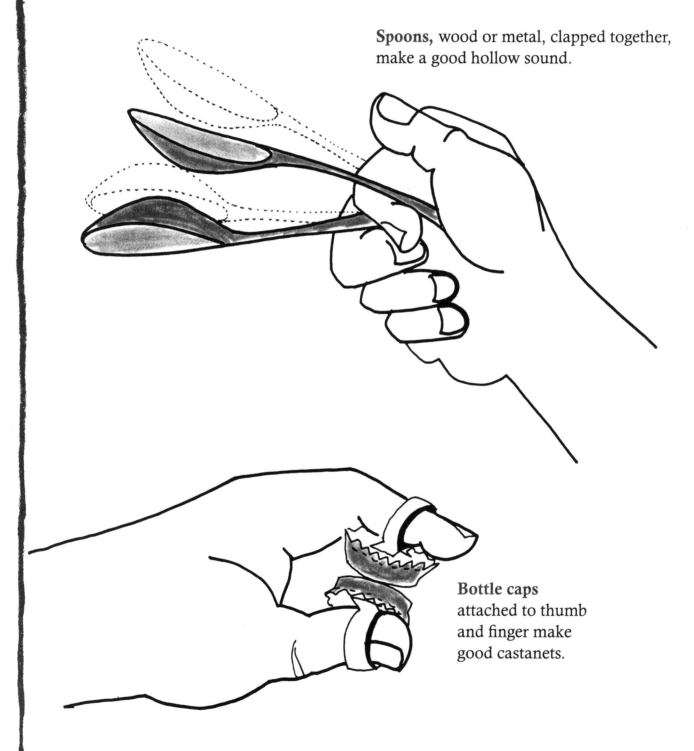

Spoons, wood or metal, clapped together, make a good hollow sound.

Bottle caps attached to thumb and finger make good castanets.

To make **walnut castanets**,
tape cloth or cardboard
finger loops onto empty shells.
Use only good shells —
a crack will spoil the tone.
Or try acorns on your fingers.

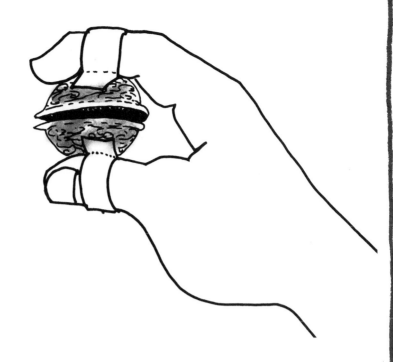

Button Castanets

Buttons, glued onto a strip
of cardboard, make a tiny
clicking sound.

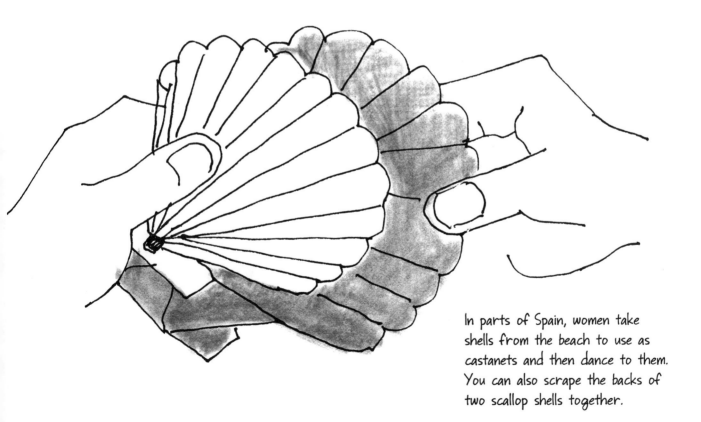

In parts of Spain, women take
shells from the beach to use as
castanets and then dance to them.
You can also scrape the backs of
two scallop shells together.

TONGUE DRUMS

An adult should help with this project.

Every wood has its own sound.
Tap a few boards and listen.
Try spruce, fruit, and
redwood for the best sounds.
At least make the top out of sonorous wood —
the rest can be pine.

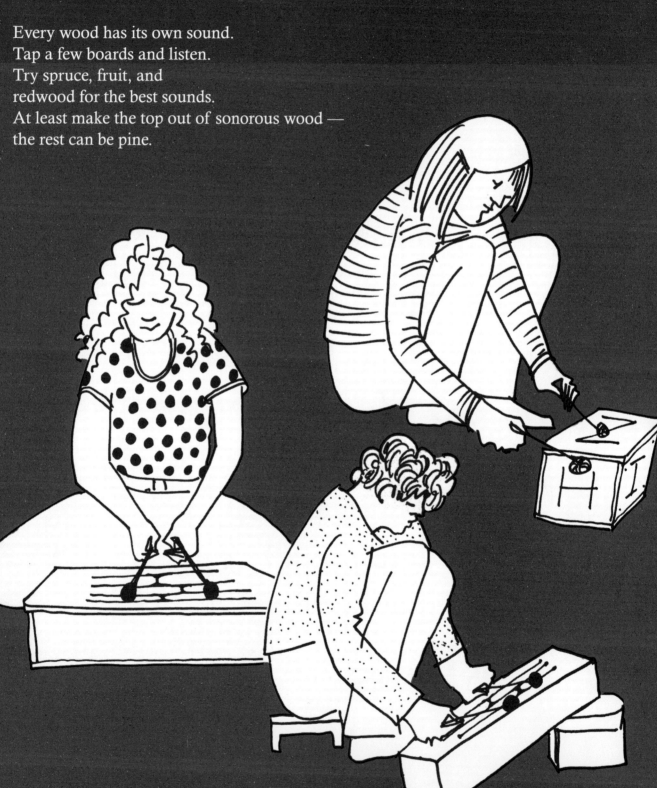

There is no magic to these measurements — use what you have on hand.
A small box will sound higher; a large box will sound deeper and richer.

Cut **top C** out of a hardwood (like redwood) 26" x 8".
Cut two sections of piece **B,** 6" x 8" (ends).
Cut two sections of piece **A,** 6" x 26" (sides).
Cut **bottom** from anything, 8" x 26".

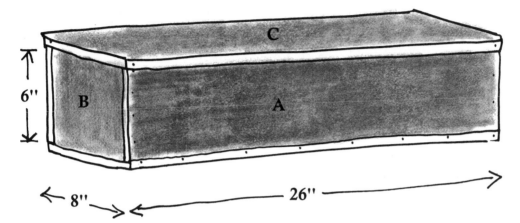

6"

B   A   C

← 8" →   26"

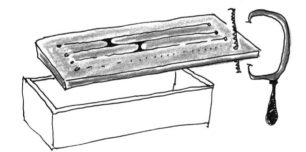

Top: Drill starting holes
and then insert the coping saw blade
to make the slits.
Cut six tongues into the top (see left),
each a different length and width.
For mallets see page 39.

HUZI X

Make a square box any size:
6" x 6" or 8" x 8" or 10" x 10".
Leave one side open.
Cut one letter
on each side.
Try H, U, Z, I, X:
each letter makes
a different sound.
Use sonorous wood
for all sides.

DRUM IMPROVISATIONS

 head

Fabric covered with white glue to size it makes a good drumhead — so do rubber bed sheets and inner tubing.

A **coffee can** with a plastic lid on one end or both makes a quick drum.

A **coconut** or **gourd** can have plastic, cloth, leather, or chamois stretched over tightly and tied.

Drums can both whisper and command. John Cage, an American composer, wrote a piece for three drums played very softly with the fingertips. You have to listen very carefully to hear it well! Try making up your own piece that sounds mysterious and quiet, then suddenly grows funny and playful, then gradually returns to that mysterious feeling.

To make sound pockets on a **steel oil drum** first heat the steel, then hammer it.

Stretch canvas or plastic over a **tin can** or **wooden bowl.** Tape it tight or tie with string or elastic.

Use a cardboard **ice cream barrel.** Stretch fabric across the top and attach it with a strong rubber band.

Empty plastic gallon **milk jugs** turned upside down make great drums.

For a two-headed drum, remove the top and bottom from the largest **tin can** you can find.
Stretch cloth, rubber, leather, or chamois over the openings.
Stitch around each head.
Lash the stitches top to bottom.

Even a **waste basket** or garbage pail with stretched canvas will work.

MALLETS

A mallet has a head; a drumstick does not.

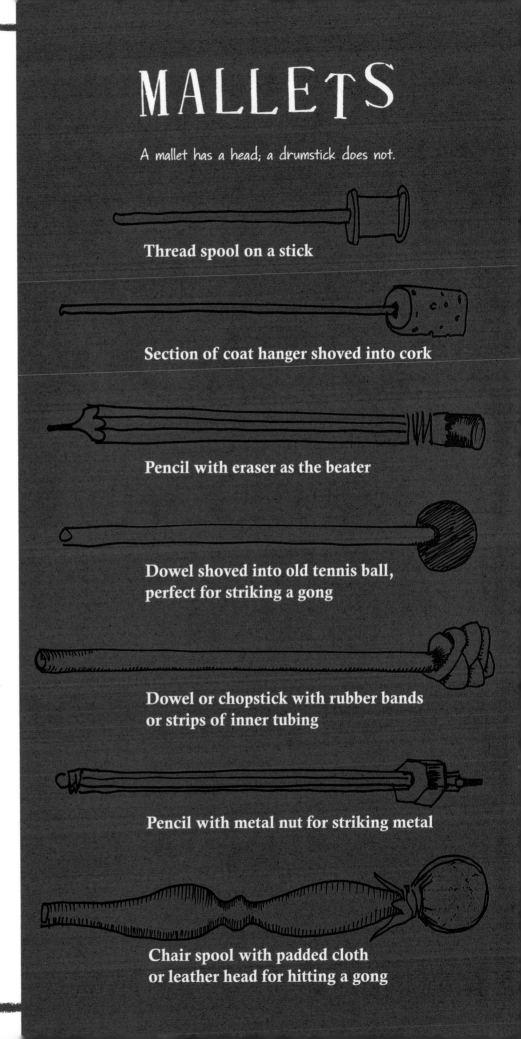

Thread spool on a stick

Section of coat hanger shoved into cork

Pencil with eraser as the beater

Dowel shoved into old tennis ball, perfect for striking a gong

Dowel or chopstick with rubber bands or strips of inner tubing

Pencil with metal nut for striking metal

Chair spool with padded cloth or leather head for hitting a gong

PLAYING
THE ROOM

With two drumsticks in hand,
explore the room,
gently striking the floor, the walls,
the blinds, the stairs.
Tap the chair, the desk,
metal cabinets, doorknobs,
bottles, wastebaskets.

Listen to your friend's sounds.
Converse with them, varying
loud and soft, fast and slow.
Imitate and improvise.
Listen — always listen as you play.
Record your percussion piece
to hear later.

Don't harm or break
anything . . . of course!

PERCUSSION CONVERSATIONS

Use instruments instead of words
to talk back and forth with a friend.
Just like speech, you can be loud or quiet,
slow or fast, high or low, funny or angry.
Always listen to your partner
as you improvise and respond.

Copy-Cat Rhythms

Someone plays a rhythm pattern.
Others copy — take turns — follow the leader —
loud and soft, fast and slow.
Include silence among your sounds.
Listen.

Silence is a vital part of music.
John Cage wrote a piece for
piano, entitled 4'33", which is
exactly 4 minutes and 33 seconds
of silence — that's all! It has
been performed many times all
over the world.

CANONS & ROUNDS

Try playing the rhythm
of a well-known canon, or round,
such as "Row, Row, Row Your Boat,"
"Frère Jacques," or "Three Blind Mice."
(You can sing it first, but then play or clap
just the rhythm of the words.)

Perform it as a canon
with a couple of other players.
The first player begins. The second player
enters when the first starts the second line.
The third player enters as the second player
starts the second line.

Play all three rounds together,
starting at the same moment.

Or tap one round on your instrument,
and have other players guess
which one it is.

Some composers write little canons for fun, as messages or puzzles to send to friends. Some can be played or sung forward, backward, and upside-down. Haydn even wrote "mirror" canons to be read with a mirror!

TALKING DRUMS

The Nigerian drummer
tucks his drum under his arm,
squeezing and relaxing the pressure
on the leather thongs
to raise or lower the pitch.
His other hand strikes the drumhead
with a curved stick.
He converses with other drummers,
changing pitches and pulses —
sometimes across long distances.

Discover all the ways you can use
your hands: tapping, clicking, rolling,
knocking, scratching, flicking, using
the fingertips, fingernails, wrists,
fists, knuckles, and palms. Play on the
wood as well as on the drumskin.

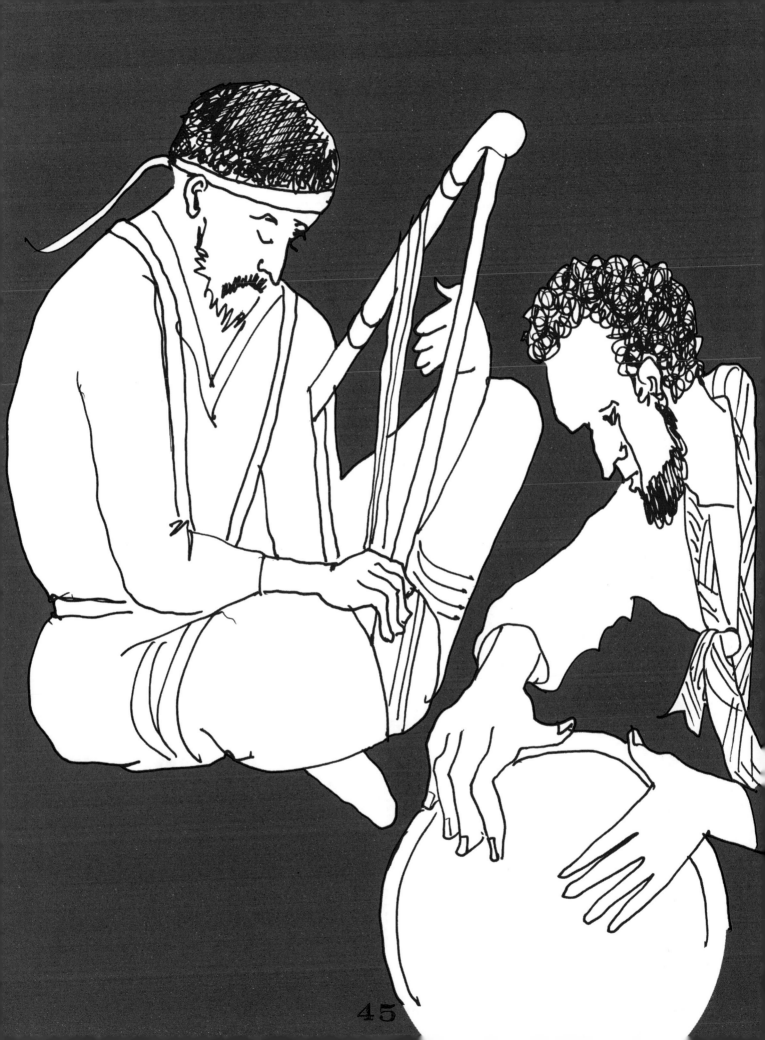

HARDWARE ORCHESTRA

Visit your neighborhood hardware store to find a wealth of musical possibilities. Here's an example: a bell you can make from a plain carbon "hole saw" blade, a metal nut, and a couple of buttons.

hole saw blade
large = 2½''
small = 1¼''

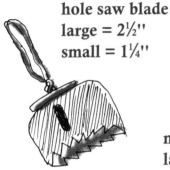

metal nut
large = ¾''
small = ¼''

two buttons

Many common things make surprising sounds. Even an ordinary identification tag becomes a whistle when you blow into the open end.

blow into this end

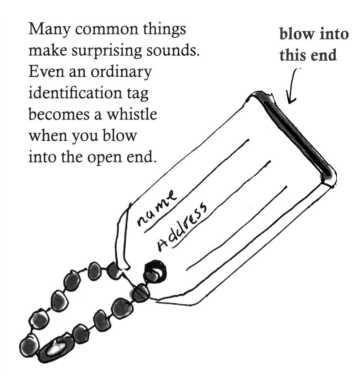

When Ann worked at the Boston Children's Museum, she and her students built a scaffolding and hung up their junk sounds. Visitors were invited to make music!

The Baschet brothers of France, a composer and a sculptor, make musical sculptures of sheet-metal pieces and standing metal rods that you can run wet fingers up and down, producing wonderful eerie sounds.

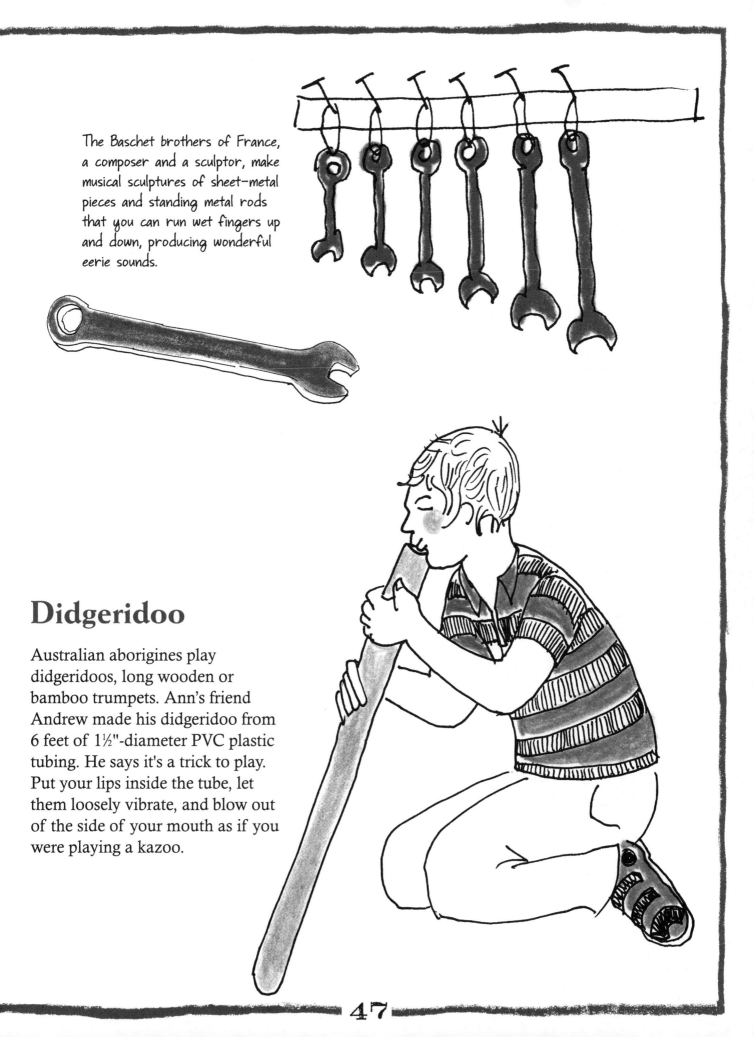

Didgeridoo

Australian aborigines play didgeridoos, long wooden or bamboo trumpets. Ann's friend Andrew made his didgeridoo from 6 feet of 1½"-diameter PVC plastic tubing. He says it's a trick to play. Put your lips inside the tube, let them loosely vibrate, and blow out of the side of your mouth as if you were playing a kazoo.

CONDUIT PIPE XYLOPHONE

An adult should help with this project.

Conduit pipe usually comes in 10' lengths.
You can buy it at the hardware store.
You will also need about 3' of felt weather
stripping to pad the bars.

Small set:
Use 10' of ½" electrical conduit pipe.
Large set:
Use 20' of ½" electrical conduit pipe.

Ask for EMT tubing, found in hardware
stores and lumberyards (copper pipe is
more expensive but easier to cut and
has a richer tone).

1 With a hacksaw, cut the longest pipe first.
In case you lose this note by cutting the bar
too short, you can use the "mistake" for the
next note and nothing is wasted. Filing the
pipe end makes the note higher in pitch.

2 Cut two 1' lengths of felt weather stripping.
Set the pipes on top of them in order of size.
Then cut eleven ½" felt divider pads. Glue
pads between pipes so pipes don't roll.

Tube Lengths

Note	Large	Small
high do	13⁷⁄₁₆"	6²²⁄₃₂"
ti	13¾"	6⅞"
la	14¾"	7⅜"
so	15⅝"	7¹³⁄₁₆"
fa	16⅝"	8⁵⁄₁₆"
mi	17⅛"	8⁹⁄₁₆"
re	18¼"	9⅛"
do	19½"	9¾"
low ti	20"	10"
low la	21¼"	10⅝"
low so	22⁷⁄₁₆"	11⁷⁄₃₂"

Reproduced from the *Musical Instrument Recipe Book* by permission of the Elementary Science Study of Education Development Center, Inc.

Table model

felt dividers

Rack made of wood,
Styrofoam, rubber,
or felt strips

Variations

Alternatively, you can cut ditches in Styrofoam blocks (**A**), make each note bar an individual cradle (**B**), or hang the pipes in a graduated series (**C**).

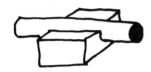

A. Styrofoam cradle

B. Individual Styrofoam pipe cradle

C. Hanging pipes

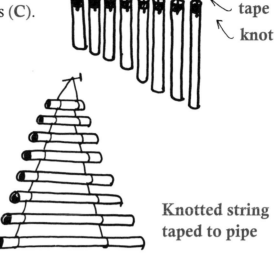

← tape

← knot

Knotted string taped to pipe

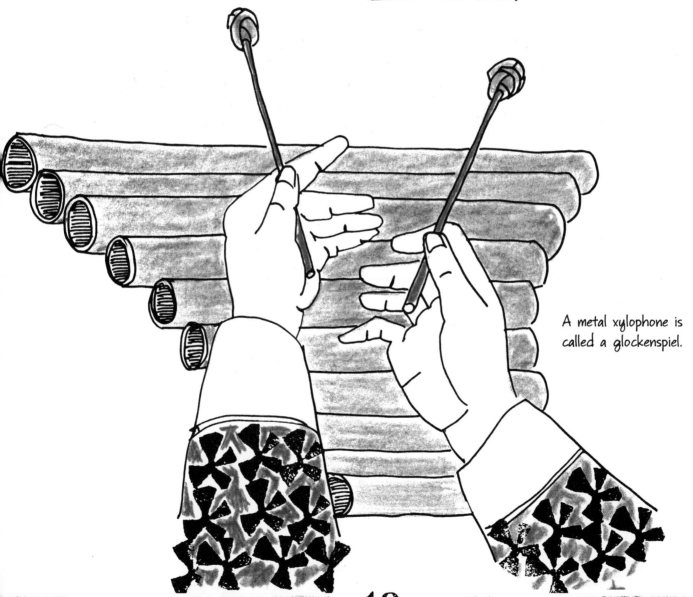

A metal xylophone is called a glockenspiel.

WOODEN XYLOPHONE

An adult should help with this project.

Some kinds of wood can really sing.
Hard, resonant woods,
such as redwood and fruitwood,
make the best tones,
but you may have to have them specially milled.
Pine is less sonorous, but much easier to find.

Use ⅞" x ⅞" strips of wood lattice.
Cut eight or more pieces at different lengths
for different pitches (see chart).
Tuning can be random or scaled.
These measurements are approximate.
To make a note higher,
sand or saw off a sliver from the end.
To lower a note,
saw a shallow notch into the block.

Make a rack to hold the note bars
out of wood or Styrofoam (**A**)
or two lengths of felt weather stripping (**B**)
on a flat surface.
Or tie your bars into a ladder.
Hang your xylophone up or lay it down.
The bars must be free in order to ring
and release their sound.

A.
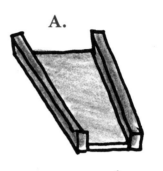
rack

B.

felt strips

Bar Measurements

Note	Length
high so	6¾"
high fa	7⅛"
high mi	7⅜"
high re	7¾"
high do	8⅜"
ti	8½"
la	9¼"
so	9⅝"
fa	10¼"
mi	10¾"
re	11½"
do	12⅛"
low ti	12⅞"
low la	13½"
low so	14¼"

The above measurements are from Ronald Roberts's book *Musical Instruments Made to Be Played,* published by Dryad Press, Woodridge, New Jersey.

The Moldavian monk sounds the plank

Tuning wooden bars can be tricky.
If you get discouraged,
why not settle for a set
of random notes . . . and invent your
own new sounds and scales.

AFRICAN THUMB PIANOS

Kalimba • Mbira

Cigar Box Mbira

Attach wires as
you see them here.
Lash them with
string or thong,
or secure them
under a strip of metal.

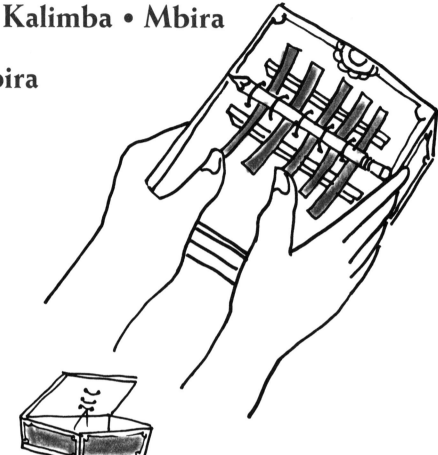

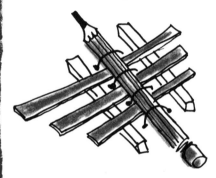

Lash the wires with string.

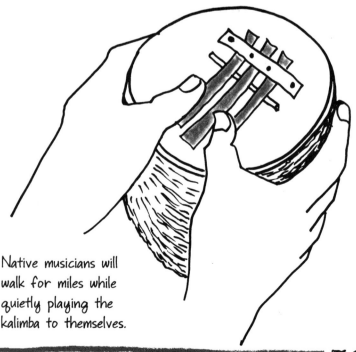

Native musicians will
walk for miles while
quietly playing the
kalimba to themselves.

An adult should help with this project.

This is how thumb pianos are made in
tropical parts of Africa, but they are
tricky to create. Eat the meat of a half-
coconut without breaking the shell.
Cut a wooden disk a little larger
than the shell opening and taper the
edges so it fits tightly into the coconut.
Wire tongues can be made out of
hammered umbrella stays
or flattened coat hanger wire
of different lengths,
or "cut-nails," flattened.

Shingle Plunker

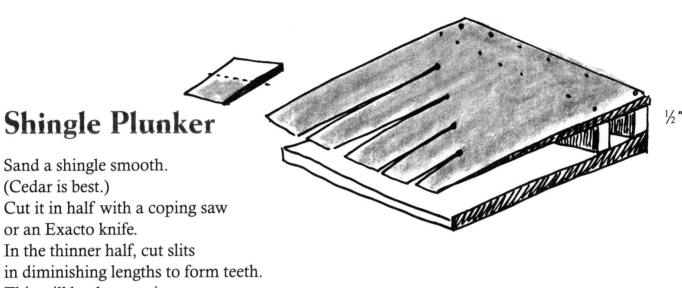

Sand a shingle smooth.
(Cedar is best.)
Cut it in half with a coping saw
or an Exacto knife.
In the thinner half, cut slits
in diminishing lengths to form teeth.
This will be the top piece.
Nail two thin strips of wood
to the thicker end of the other piece of shingle.
Nail thin top piece to cross bars as shown.

½"

Tongue Depressor Mbira

You need seven tongue depressors and two clamps or binder clips.
Clamp two tongue depressors across the other five, which should be
arranged so they protrude at different lengths to make different pitches.

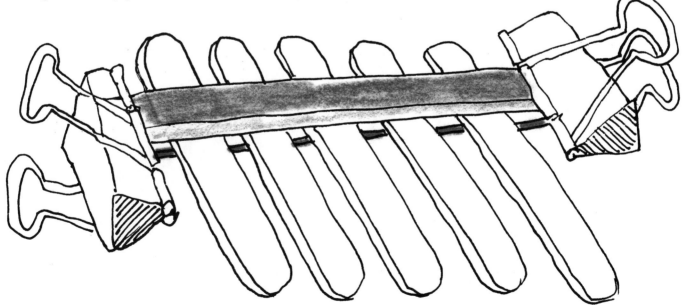

BUGLES & HORNS

Ann heard someone actually play "Joy to the World" on this tube!

1 You'll need one or more yards of **shower hose** or **flexible tubing.**

2 Make a mouthpiece from a **shower bulb** (better yet, find a mouthpiece from an old trumpet).

3 Use a **plastic funnel** for the "bell."

Attach funnel and mouthpiece to either end of hose. Blow into mouthpiece, buzzing with your lips to make a good sound.

Wind Tube

Different lengths of plastic pool tubing (1" diameter) when swung around and around fast make many notes . . . an amazing sound.

RANDOM PIPES

Cut a bunch of plastic straws
into different lengths
or use ½"–¾" plastic tubing
or cane cut in random lengths.
Plug the bottoms of the tubes
with non-drying plastic clay —
the higher you put the plug,
the higher the note.
(Push in plug with a pencil or nail head.)
Lash pipes together as the shepherds do
with string, tape, or thong.

Blow across the tops.
(It takes a little practice.)

To tune the notes better,
you can adjust the clay plug.

short tubes = high notes
long tubes = low notes

Pipe Measurements

If you want to get close to a
proper Western scale, try:

Note	Length
do	12"
re	11"
mi	10"
fa	10"
so	9"
la	9"
ti	8"
do	8"

1 With scissors, cut three pieces
of garden hose, each 5" long.

2 Plug one piece with plastic clay at end.
Plug second piece at 4" length.
Plug third piece at 3" length.
(Use a pencil to push in the clay.)

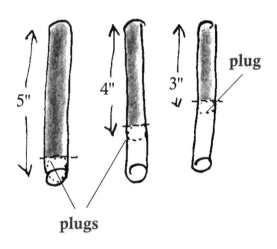

plugs

3 Lay pipes on two strips of masking
tape. Put a pinch of clay between
each pipe. Then wrap tape around.
Blow across the top.

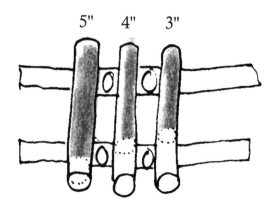

When you listen to recorded music, choose your favorite instrument and join right in.

Box Pipes

Try diminishing sizes of plastic straws.
Stick straws in a section of
corrugated box.
Glue straws in place.
Tape bottoms shut or plug with plastic clay.

Test-Tube Pipes

Diminish the water
to vary the tones.
(Add food coloring
so small people can play a tune
by reading a color chart.)

FLUTES & WHISTLES

Pipes, whistles, and flutes
can be made out of bamboo,
cane, plastic drinking straws,
garden hose, papier-mâché,
and empty ballpoint pen tubes.

Remember,
primitive pipes
come in all sizes
with unscaled notes.
With that freedom,
you can explore sound
that tickles the ears.

SHEPHERD'S PIPE

An adult should help with this project.

Use a section of bamboo about 11½" long x ¾" or ⅞" diameter or try plastic pipe or a papier-mâché tube formed around a broomstick.

Find or shape a cork that fits the opening. Drill finger holes as shown. Don't forget the wind hole and the thumb hole on the back directly behind the top finger hole.

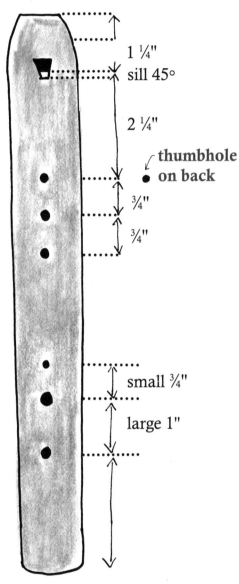

1 ¼"

sill 45°

2 ¼"

thumbhole on back

¾"

¾"

small ¾"

large 1"

Interior diameter ¾"-⅞"

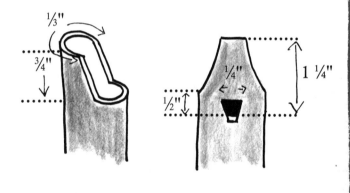

⅓"

¾"

¼"

½"

1 ¼"

wind hole

Cut the cork.

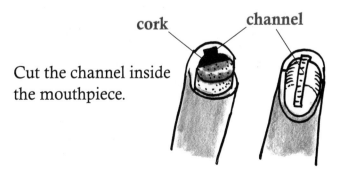

cork   channel

Cut the channel inside the mouthpiece.

DANDELION TRUMPETS

Why are we so mean
to dandelions?
I think them beautiful and wild,
and they can make MUSIC!

1 Find a long (5" or taller),
strong, fat dandelion stem.

2 Snip off the flower.

3 Split the top of the stem with your
thumbnail.

4 Pinch the top of the stem to make
a flat mouthpiece.

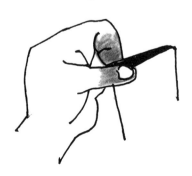

5 Nick finger holes with
your fingernail to make
different pitches.

6 Blow with lips closed.

If you can't make a sound at first, put a little more of
the stem into your mouth (up to an inch), or shorten
the stem. Buzz with your lips until you get a good
sound. The dandelion may last an hour before it wilts.

WINDOW WIND HARP

Could this be the sound
of the ancient Aeolian harp?
Make a box as wide as your window.
Build a 2" vertical edge on each end.
Put six to ten screw-eyes at either end,
and string fishing line tightly across;
or make holes and tie the strings
to nails as shown.
Make two 1" bridges and place them
under the strings to tighten.
(If you can tune the strings
to exactly the same pitch,
a strong wind will give you the great
harmonic sound of the spheres.)
Set the harp in your window
on a windy day, half in and half out,
to catch the breeze.
Let the window frame hold it in place.
Listen to the song of the wind.

bridge

Aeolus was the Greek
god of the winds.

BOARD & BOX ZITHER

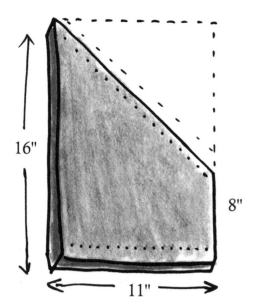

An adult should help with these projects.

The Simple Board Zither

Cut a 1" board 16" x 11" x 8" as shown.
Along the bottom, starting 1" in from left side,
mark dots with pencil every ½", for nails.
At top, along the angle,
mark dots every ¾",
for screw-eye string tighteners.
Attach 1" nails and screw-eyes
and string them with fishing line.

The Box Zither

Make a thin wooden box (16" x 11" x 8"),
using sonorous wood like cherry,
redwood, maple, cedar, or spruce,
for the sounding board top.
The rest of the box can be anything
you happen to have handy, like pine.
Cut a sound hole
approximately 3" in diameter
in the lower center of the box.
Cut two strips of wood —
a 13½" strip for the top to hold
the screw-eye string tighteners
and an 11" strip
for the bottom string holder.
Glue strips to sounding board.
String with guitar gut,
fishing line, or nylon monofilament.
Tune with the help of a piano.

You can also make
a three-octave zither
or a four-octave table model.

Top 13½ " string tightener

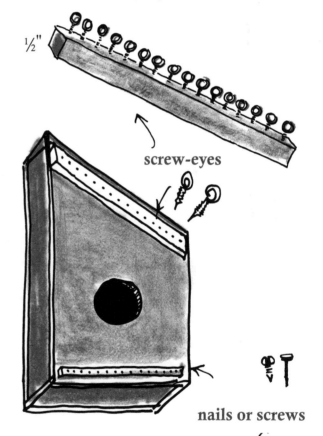

½"

screw-eyes

nails or screws

Bottom 11" string holder

½"

63

ONE STRING
BOX BASS

An adult should help with this project.

Find or make a box.
Cut a bridge.
Make a slot in the bridge for the string.
Glue it on about midway.
Cut sound hole at lower end of boxtop.
Cut **holes A and B** for stick neck
to pass through *tightly!*

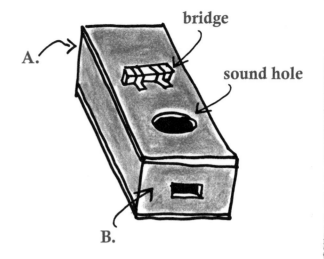

bridge

A.

sound hole

B.

stick neck

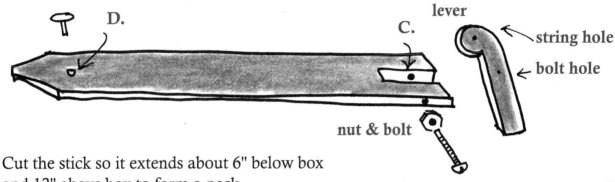

D.

C.

lever

string hole

bolt hole

nut & bolt

Cut the stick so it extends about 6" below box
and 12" above box to form a neck,
or make a floor-to-shoulder standing bass stem
and place the sound box to suit your height.
Cut slot for lever quite snug.
Drill holes through neck **(C)** for a bolt.
Cut lever and drill hole in it for the bolt
and a hole for a string.
Drill hole at **(D)** for peg,
or just put a screw there.
Tie string from lever to peg.
Pull down lever handle to change sound
and pluck or use bow for different sounds.

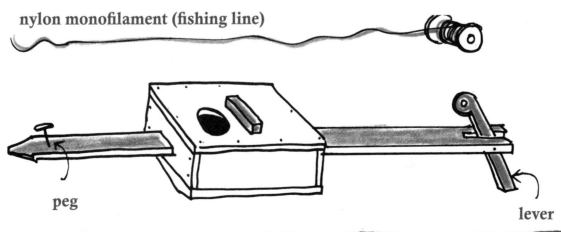

nylon monofilament (fishing line)

peg

lever

BUSHMAN'S BOW • LYRE
RUBBER BAND BOX

The Bushmen
of the Kalihari
make their bows sing
by tapping
an arrow shaft
against the string.

Rubber bands sing
across a firm box.
Two pencils will make a bridge.

Invent your own lyre.
Try a Y branch
for plucking,
bowing, or tapping.
For string,
use strips of
stretched rubber bands,
fishing line,
or nylon monofilament.

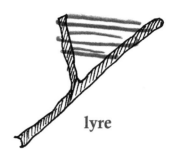

lyre

Wrap rubber bands or straps
around the back or legs of a chair
and strum.

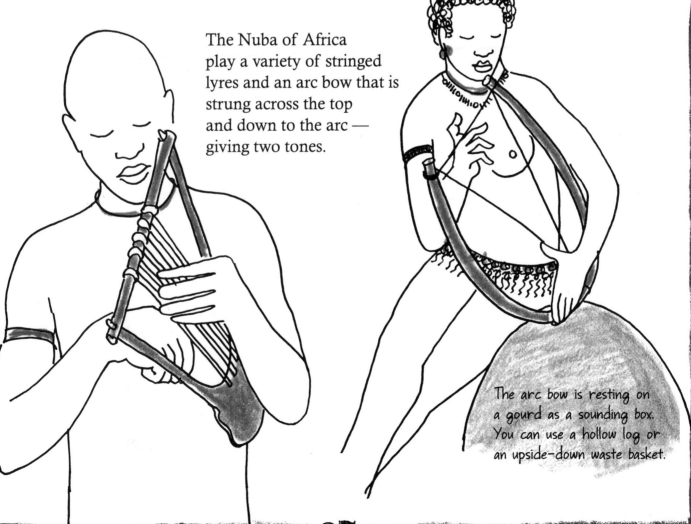

The Nuba of Africa
play a variety of stringed
lyres and an arc bow that is
strung across the top
and down to the arc —
giving two tones.

The arc bow is resting on
a gourd as a sounding box.
You can use a hollow log or
an upside-down waste basket.

MILK CARTON GUITAR

An adult should help with this project.

All you need is a yardstick, a milk carton, six screw-eyes, a knife, and some fishing line.

1 Cut an H-shaped hole the width of the stick in the milk carton about 1" from the "roof."

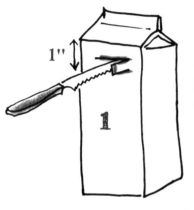

If you cut this shape, it will hold the stick more tightly when you poke it through.

3 Attach the screw-eyes to both ends of the yardstick. Tie each string tightly to one screw-eye, insert it through the slot, and tie it to the opposite screw-eye.

2 Cut slots for strings.

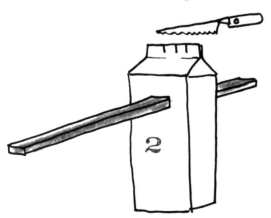

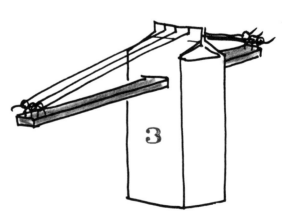

HOMOGENIZED

MILK

To keep a knot in monofilament line from slipping, touch it with a hot match to melt it.

The screw-eyes provide you with a way to tighten the strings.

To play: strum, tap, or use an old violin bow.

An even simpler guitar is the one-string board and cup.

PLUCKING FIDDLE

An adult should help with this project.

This fiddle has a lovely sound.
By pressing the string down
with your thumb,
you can get many very clear notes.

You need a plastic jug,
a long stick about ¾" x 24" or more
(a yardstick is fine),
two screw-eyes, and
a small block of wood
to serve as a bridge
(a pencil will do).

1 Saw a little ditch in the middle of the block or pencil to cradle the string, which can be fishing line, gut guitar string, or nylon monofilament.

2 To make sure the stick is tight, cut slits in this shape about 1" from the bottom of the jug. Poke the stick through.

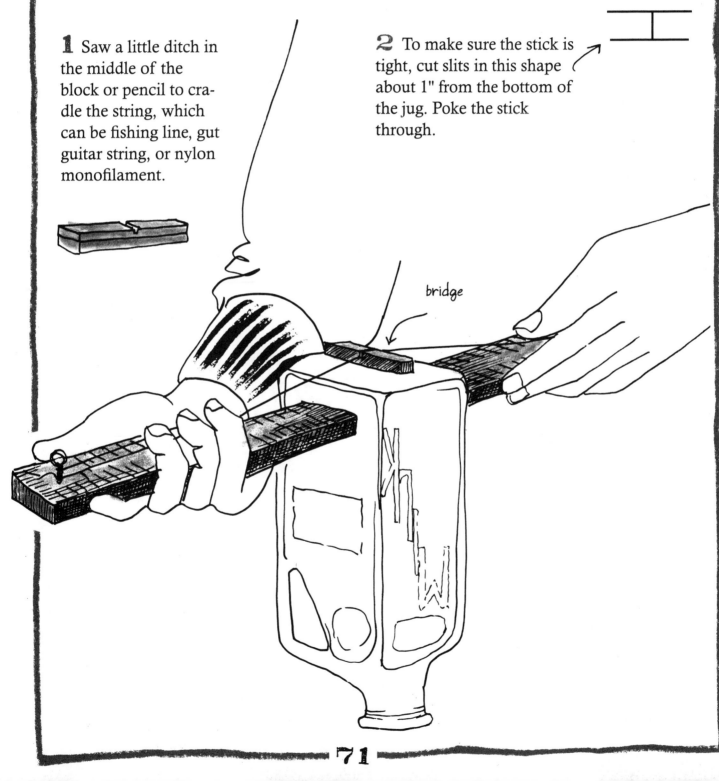

bridge

MUSICAL SAW

The common house saw (28" or 30")
(for cutting wood)
makes beautiful music
when a bow is drawn
against the toothless edge.
As you raise and lower
the blade, it cries
high and low sounds.

We ordered
a toothless saw directly
from the manufacturer
(check on the Internet).
The sound is the same,
with teeth or without.

Ann's father once played his musical saw in
Steinway Hall in New York City. The Reviewer
said Mr. Wiseman played his "utensil" with skill.
It was a voice & piano solo with saw obligato.

Strong bent stick

It's best to use an old violin bow, if you can find one. A bow is very difficult to make, requiring 50 to 100 strands of linen thread, monofilament, or hairs from a horse tail, knotted at both ends.

You can buy rosin at most music stores to rub on bow strings to make them sing.

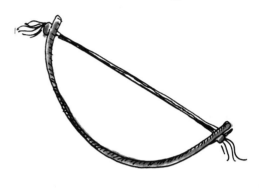

Notch at both ends —
either way

1 Place the saw handle flat on your thigh, so the smooth edge of the blade faces away from you.

2 Cross your other leg over to clamp the saw firmly.

3 Place your thumb about 3" from the tip and bend an S-curve in the saw blade.   S-curve
Raise the blade up and down, changing the curve in the saw until you find the sounds you want.

4 To play, stroke the saw edge firmly with a violin bow, or draw the bow hard against the curved blade. The voice of the blade is better in certain areas.

5 If you don't have a violin bow, you can tap with a stick as you raise the blade up and down, but you'll get no vibration.

6 The sound varies with the pressure of bow stroke. A 28" saw will give six or seven notes; a 30" saw will give a full octave.

CONDUCTING AN ORCHESTRA

Choose someone to be the conductor,
to decide which instrument should play when.

Point to others, bring more in,
combine different sounds, thin them out.
Make moments of magical silence.
Conduct the orchestra to an ending.

Take turns as conductor.
Record a performance to play back later.

Before beginning, the conductor has to
listen to each instrument to know its sound.
Each sound is like a color. There must be
absolute silence at the start, just like a blank
canvas. Then the conductor points to the
first sound. What will it be?

KITCHEN CONCERTO

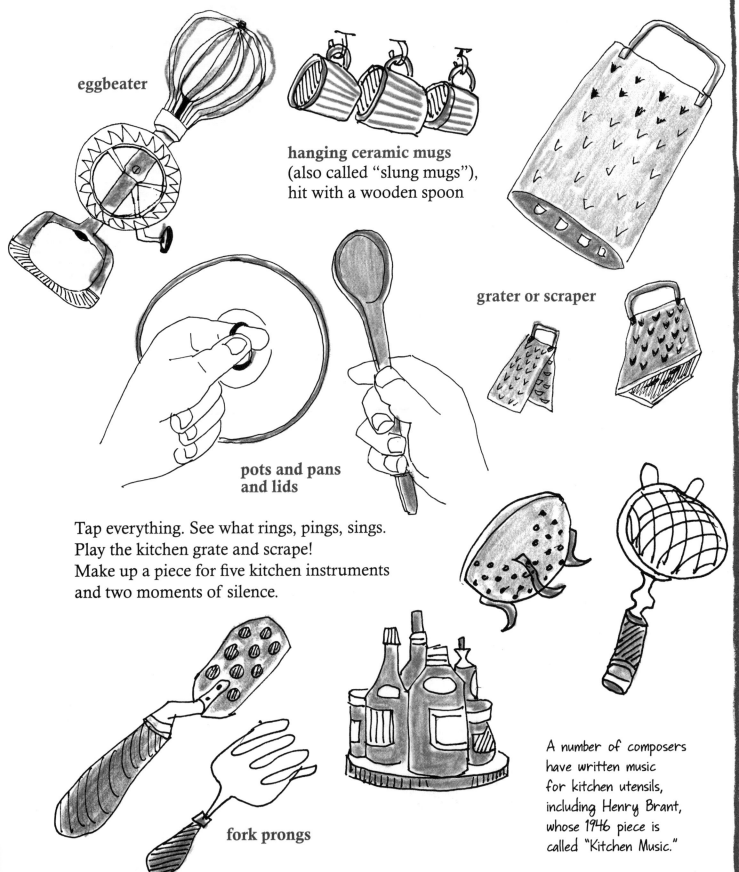

eggbeater

hanging ceramic mugs
(also called "slung mugs"),
hit with a wooden spoon

grater or scraper

pots and pans
and lids

Tap everything. See what rings, pings, sings.
Play the kitchen grate and scrape!
Make up a piece for five kitchen instruments
and two moments of silence.

fork prongs

A number of composers
have written music
for kitchen utensils,
including Henry Brant,
whose 1946 piece is
called "Kitchen Music."

A PRE-HISPANIC ORCHESTRA

Seedpod rattles

Wooden rainsticks in many shapes, often that of a snake

Tree trunk drum

Tortoise shell, played with deer antlers or sticks

Tongue or slit drums, a type of xylophone made from hollow logs

gourd drum

The earliest instruments date from approximately 8000 B.C. Members of the Children's Pre-Hispanic Orchestra in San Miguel de Allende, Mexico, play authentic copies of these ancient instruments. The orchestra, with children ages 9 to 16, is called *Collar del Viento* (the Wind's Necklace).

Ceremonial drum, struck with hands or mallet, usually carved from a log with a skin stretched tightly over the top

Clay flute

Conch shell trumpet

Rasps from bone or wood, scraped with deer antler or stick

Ehecatl

Musical stones (xylophone) played with two small stones

PAPER ORCHESTRA

Give each player sheets of newspaper,
a magazine, or a small paper bag.
LISTEN as you
rip, tear, rattle,
shake, crumple, twist, snap,
and then pop the paper bag
with a final bang.
Take turns conducting.

. . . .

Make an orchestra of WOOD sounds:
Claves, maracas, quiros,
slit drums, and acorn finger tappers.
Make an orchestra of METAL sounds:
Cymbals, bells, chimes, pots, pipes,
jangling keys, and jingling johnnies.

CLOCK MUSIC

Opus 2: Paper and Water

A full clock music score consists of:

1 A large drawing of a clock face on which different colors and graphic notations indicate exactly when, over the course of a minute, every sound or instrument will play.

2 A key showing which sound or instrument each notation represents, listed below the score.

You will also need a real clock with a second hand. The second hand acts as the conductor. The players take their cues from the sweep of the second hand as it points to each second on the perimeter of the clock.

Make a small, individual score for each player, showing only his or her part. Each person watches the "conductor" — the second hand on the real clock — and plays from his or her score when the time is right.

sandpaper = ●●●
scrunch paper = ◆◆◆
bubbling water = ✷✷✷
tap water glasses, starting very softly and growing louder = ✛✛✛
paper bag – blown up to pop! = ❗
Rip newspapers in short or long bursts = ✦✦✦

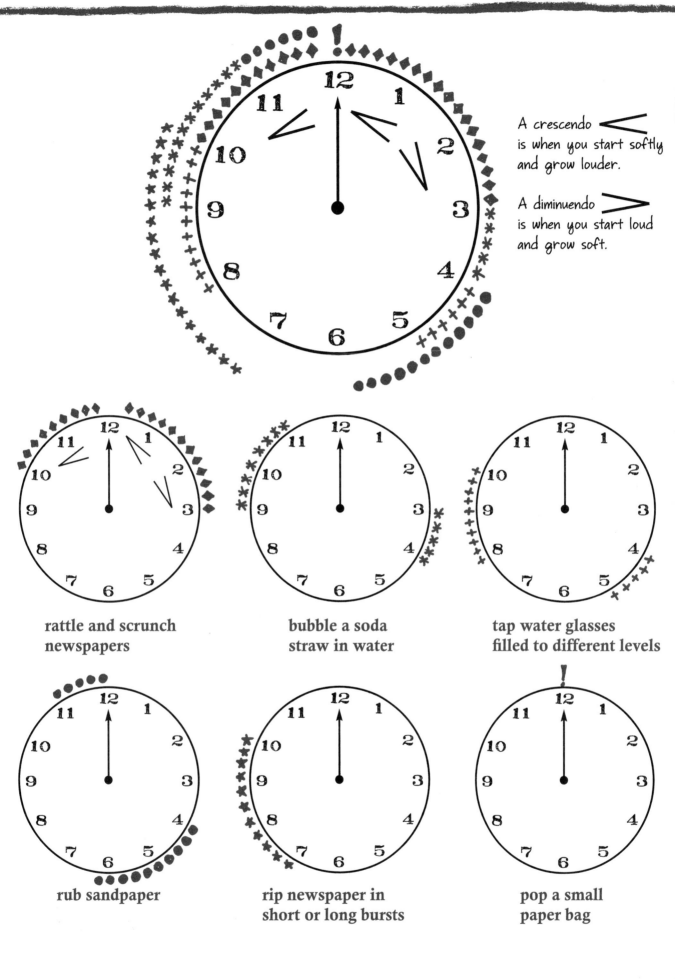

A crescendo ⟨ is when you start softly and grow louder.

A diminuendo ⟩ is when you start loud and grow soft.

rattle and scrunch newspapers

bubble a soda straw in water

tap water glasses filled to different levels

rub sandpaper

rip newspaper in short or long bursts

pop a small paper bag

CLOCK MUSIC

Opus 3: Anything Goes

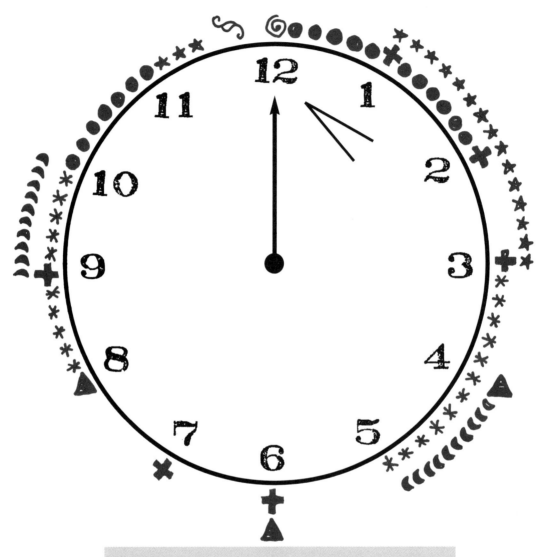

On this score you can substitute other instruments.

Seed pods, maracas, shakers = ●●●
Drum (only one beat) = ✚
Claves, guiro, seashells = ★★★
Bells = ◗◗◗
Kalimba, glockenspiel, xylophone = ✴✴✴
Rainstick (let fall only once) = §
Triangle, cowbell (one tap) = ▲
Gong, cymbal (with one soft stick) = ◉

Now make up your own scores and play them with your friends.

SOUNDSCAPES

You've seen a landscape —
what about a soundscape you can hear?
Let instruments tell the story of a storm
or a summer meadow,
going from stillness to sound
and back to stillness.
Like this —
Rain starts to fall softly,
gradually growing louder;
winds begin to blow,
howl and whistle.
Distant thunder rumbles, crashes.
As the storm passes,
everything reverses,
quiets down,
returns to silence.

Choose a story
to tell in sounds.
Create your own soundscape
with instruments and objects,
clapping hands, and weird voices.

Make seashore sounds
or city noises,
a spooky Halloween night,
birds calling, frogs croaking,
dogs barking in the distance.
Record your soundscapes.

 **Draw a picture of a scene and then bring it to life with sound.**

Here are some possible sounds and how to make them.

wind: **thin-rimmed glass**
wailing wind: **handsaw with bow**
rain: **thimble fingers**
heavy rain: **slung mugs**
buoy: **triangle**
storm: **scallop shells**
deep sea, distant thunder: **large PVC thumping pipes**
insects: **guiro, maracas, or shaker**
spring peepers: **small bells**
woodpecker: **wood block**

Benjamin Britten used mugs tuned to different pitches and hung from strings in his children's opera *Noye's Fludde.* He called these "slung mugs." The player struck them with a wooden spoon to create the sound of the first raindrops hitting the Ark.

VELCRO - ZIPPER DUETS

Zippers and Velcro
on jackets and shoes
zapped and zipped
make sounds you can use
for a jazzy duet.

Make up a composition:
short and long strokes,
fast and slow,
solo and together.
Create patterns —
talk back and forth.

Use a duffel bag or sleeping bag zipper to make a long, slow sound.

SINGLE-NOTE COMPOSITIONS

Make up a musical piece,
using only *one* note.
How will you start?
What will happen?
How will your single-note piece end?

You can do this on any instrument,
or try this.
Stretch a big elastic band across
the knobs of a chair.
Strum the string.
Repeat the note,
soft and loud,
slow and fast.
Make spaces of silence between notes.

This is one of the most difficult things for a composer
or a musician: to take one note and make it interesting.

ORCHESTRATING

Orchestrate the words of a song or a poem that grows longer and longer. Bring in a different percussion instrument to accompany each new addition to this well-known story.
Never slow the rhythm. It's tricky!

"This is the house that Jack built. [All instruments play together, called *tutti*.]

"This is the malt [solo instrument] that lay in the house that Jack built [all, *tutti*].

"This is the rat [another solo instrument] that ate the malt [solo from first verse] that lay in the house that Jack built *[tutti]*.

"This is the cat [a different instrument] that killed the rat [solo] that ate the malt [solo] that lay in the house that Jack built *[tutti]*.

"This is the dog [continue as before] that worried the cat, that killed the rat, that ate the malt that lay in the house that Jack built.

"This is the cow with the crumpled horn, that tossed the dog, that worried the cat . . . [continue with the rest of the lines] that lay in the house that Jack built.

"This is the maiden all forlorn, that milked the cow with the crumpled horn, that tossed the dog . . . [etc.] that lay in the house that Jack built.

"This is the man all tattered and torn, that kissed the maiden all forlorn, that milked the cow with the crumpled horn, that tossed the dog, that worried the cat, that killed the rat, that ate the malt that lay in the house that Jack built."

Afterward, play this story all the way through on instruments alone, without words. WOW!

Other pieces that "accumulate" include "This Old Man," "The 12 Days of Christmas," "The Tree in the Wood," "The Rattlin' Bog," "Old MacDonald Had a Farm," "Chad Gad Yo," and "Alouette."

CLAPPING AND BODY DRUMMING

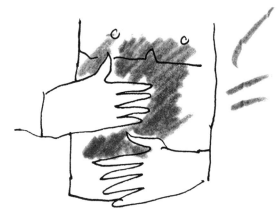

Were hands, voice, and feet
our first instruments?
Hands can make different sounds
depending on how
you put them together.

Body Drumming

slapping thighs
clicking heels
tapping toes
beating chest
patting cheeks full of air
Create a symphony of BODY SOUNDS.
Make up a symbol for each sound.
Write a clock score for ten players.

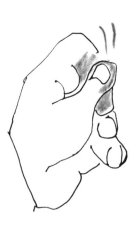

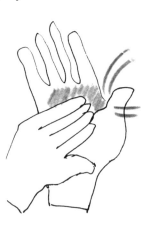

open palms   cupped palms   snapping, flicking   rubbing

CLOCK MUSIC

OPUS 4: Body Language

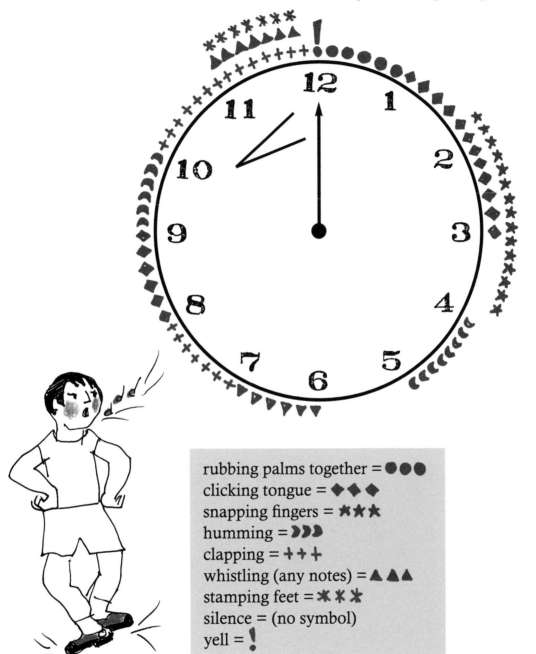

rubbing palms together = ●●●
clicking tongue = ◆◆◆
snapping fingers = ★★★
humming = ❱❱❱
clapping = +++
whistling (any notes) = ▲▲▲
stamping feet = ✳✳✳
silence = (no symbol)
yell = !

Percussive Feet

See how many different sounds you can make with your feet. Start very slowly and softly, getting faster and louder, until you are doing a very loud, fast and furious-sounding percussion piece. Then slow down until you can barely be heard. Try it alone or with friends.

FAMILY FUN

Clap your hands
slap your knees
blow the bottle
shake the keys.
Thump the chair
strum the bow
beat the pans
tap your toes.

Choose a conductor
to lead the group.
Give everyone a turn
as conductor.

Play together
or play alone,
loud or soft,
the conductor's choice.
Record your piece,
play it back;
try again
till you get the knack.

End Notes

Toward the end of one of my teaching videos, I ask the children, "What is music?"

They sit there thinking, silent, as they wonder what I was asking. We had spent two weeks together discovering what pitch, rhythm, dynamics, phrasing, canons, drones, harmony, composing, and conducting meant.

No answer.

I urge them on. "I know you know it! Don't think so hard, just say the first thing that comes into your head! Go back to our earliest thoughts about how music began."

Long pause.

Suddenly a hand flies up above the group, and Rebecca exclaims, "Sound! Sounds."

"Yes," I respond, elated at the answer. Going on (for here was my chance), I ask, "And what is the opposite of sound?"

Not a word, everyone thinking hard. Finally Pedro murmurs, "Quiet?" which prompts another voice to say "Silence."

"Yes, exactly. That's it!" I say. "You've got it! Sound and silence."

I couldn't have been more pleased.

— J.L.

When I think about music, I am amazed at the way it affects people's emotions, how it lets people's feelings out and makes them dance.

When I think about instruments, I see my dad stroking his musical saw, making it cry the mournful tune "Drink to Me Only With Thine Eyes." I see a lonesome man pouring his soul into his mouth organ, cupped between his hands, making it cry and laugh, making it moan. I see the music student I roomed with in Paris years ago hugging her viola da gamba, carrying it all over Paris, strapped to her back. I see my little son, not yet one, with a spoon and a pot making a sound all his own. I see a girl with a tin pennywhistle playing Irish ballads that break your heart at the sound of "Oh Danny Boy, the pipes, the pipes are calling . . . ."

Every spring a woman sets up her glass harp in Harvard Square, letting spectators turn the wheel as she plays "Jesu Joy Of Man's Desiring" with her fingers on the wet glass. Nearby, a Chinese man plays a two-string bamboo instrument with a thin bamboo bow, making sounds very foreign to our Western ears. But it's clear he's in love with these sounds, as the strings cry strange notes under his quick strokes.

I think everyone needs an instrument, like an extra voice that lets the feelings out when words are not enough.

I hope when you finish making instruments from these pages that you will find one you love and teach it the language of your heart. Then you will always have a secret friend.

— A.S.W.

Helpful Musical Terms

Canon. A round; a musical piece in which two or more parts all have exactly the same melody but start at different times

Crescendo. Starting soft and growing louder

Diminuendo. Starting loud and growing softer

Dynamics. Loudness and softness

Polyrhythms. Combination of different rhythms, all played at once

Syncopation. Temporarily changing the accent in a musical passage so as to emphasize the weak beat

Tempo. The speed of a piece

Resources

Music to Listen to

Having made our own music with this book, we can also hear how some of these same simple ideas are used by composers of sophisticated, serious music. It's easy to locate any of these composers on the Internet and, in many cases, actually to hear some of their percussion ensemble pieces on line: the Baschet brothers, Luciano Berio, Pierre Boulez, Henry Brant, Earle Brown, Carlos Chavez, Henry Cowell, Lou Harrison, Alan Hovhaness, Luigi Nono, Carl Orff, Harry Partch, Gunther Schuller, Karl-Heinz Stockhausen, and Edgar Varese.

Here are the composers and pieces mentioned in this book, as well as some others of interest:

Benjamin Britten. *Noye's Fludde* (1958)

Henry Brant. *Kitchen Music* (1946) and other works

Carlos Chavez. *Toccata for Percussion* (1942) and other works

John Cage. "4'33"" (1952); *Amores* (1943; one movement is for quiet drums)

Franz Josef Haydn. *Symphony no. 47 in G major.* In the third movement, each section of the score is followed by its exact mirror image.

Tim Hazell. *Collar del Viento,* the Children's Pre-Hispanic Orchestra (see Website address below).

Wolfgang Amadeus Mozart. *Adagio for glass harmonica in C major, K. 356* (K. 617a); *Adagio and Rondo for glass harmonica, flute, oboe, viola & cello in C minor, K. 617*

Harry Partch. Numerous works for cloud chamber bowls, gourd tree with gongs, and more, including *Cloud-Chamber Music* and *Ring Around the Moon* (both 1949–50).

Karl-Heinz Stockhausen. *Zyklus for Percussion* (1959). A solo percussion piece for nine instruments. The score is written so that the performance can start on any page, and it can be read upside down, or from right to left, as the performer chooses.

Other Sources

Janice Allen, et al., *Meet Me at the Garden Gate* (Hartford, CT: Kodaly Institute, 1984). Includes street chants as rhythmic musical pieces.

James Blades, *Percussion Instruments and Their History* (London: Faber and Faber Ltd. 1970, 1974). Definitive and fascinating resource volume written by the great English percussionist.

Elementary Science Study of Education Development Center, Inc. *Musical Instrument Recipe Book* (Watertown, MA).

Margaret Galloway. *Making and Playing Bamboo Pipes* (Woodbridge, New Jersey: Dryad Press). Instructions on making precise bamboo pipes. Now out of print, but worth a search in a used-book store.

John Hawkinson. *Music and Instruments for Children to Make* (Albert Whitman & Co., 1969).

John Langstaff. *Songs for Singing Children* (Watertown, MA: Revels, 2003). A compact disc recording of children making music with

John Langstaff, including percussion instruments they play as part of the orchestra.

Nancy and John Langstaff. *Sally Go Round the Moon* (Watertown, MA: Revels 1986). A collection of songs and singing games that can be played on pitched and non-pitched percussion instruments, some in a single rhythmic pattern (as drone, or *ostinato*), others as melodic lines.

Ronald Roberts. *Musical Instruments Made to Be Played* (Woodridge, New Jersey: Dryad Press; republished by David & Charles, 1976).

R. Murray Schafer. *The Thinking Ear* (Toronto: Arcana Editions, 1988). Schafer's writings on music education include several of our thoughts in this book, and he has been a great inspiration to many musicians and teachers.

Stevens, Bryna. *Ben Franklin's Glass Armonica* (Minneapolis: Carolrhoda Books, 1983). Illustrated by Priscilla Kiedrowski. The story of Franklin's fascinating invention.

Ann Sayre Wiseman, *Making Things: A Handbook of Creative Discovery* (Little Brown & Co., 1997). Dozens of useful and creative projects. Check Ann's Website (below) for more of her books.

Videotapes

How to Play the Didgeridoo (Australian Bushcraft Library, 1996). Chris Adnam. P.O. Box 19, Hopetoun Gardens, Elsternwick, Victoria, 3185, Australia; or bushcrft@ozemail.com.au

Let's Sing! (Berkeley, CA: Langstaff Video Project, 1998). John Langstaff teaches children (ages 3 to 7) songs with their own accompanying percussion.

Let's Keep Singing! (Berkeley, CA: Langstaff Video Project, 1998). John Langstaff teaches children (ages 8 to 10) songs with their own accompanying percussion, including clock music.

Stomp Out Loud! (HBO Studios, 1998). Directed by Luke Cresswell and Steve McNicholas. A video recording of the amazing percussion group that makes music and theatre using ordinary found objects (see Website address below).

Websites

www.annsayrewiseman.com. Visit Ann's Website to learn more about her art, life, books, courses, and travels.

www.bangonacan.com. Check out this organization of performers, composers, and producers dedicated entirely to "adventurous contemporary music" using ordinary and extraordinary sounds.

www.musicalsaw.com. Learn about, listen to, and order a musical saw.

www.glassarmonica.com. Site devoted to the glass harmonica or "armonica."

www.harpmaker.net/windharp.htm. Information about and sales of Aeolian harps.

members.aol.com/woinem1/index. Musical instruments that use the wind.

www.geocities.com/Vienna/Strasse/7353/Aeolian. Information on the Aeolian harp.

www.amwoodinc.com Wooden parts for instruments.

www.elderly.com/vintage. Used violin bows.

aboriginalart.com.au/didgeridoo/dig_back ground.html. Enter the world of the Australian Aboriginal didgeridoo. See also: **www.well.com/user/nhunter/didj/**

www.stomponline.com. A performing percussion group that drums on and with ordinary found objects such as hubcaps, pipes, street signs, and plastic garbage pails.

Experimental Musical Instruments at www.wind world.com/emi. Information on the design, construction, and enjoyment of unusual sound sources ranging from Styrofoam cellos to driftwood marimbas.

www.gemueseorchester.org This "vegetable orchestra," based in Vienna, Austria, makes instruments from vegetables (such as a carrot flute), plays them (everything from classical music to traditional African music), and then cooks them into a soup for the audience.

www.timhazell.com. Here you can find information on *Collar del Viento,* the Children's Pre-Hispanic Orchestra in San Miguel de Allende, Mexico. To order their CD, write Tim Hazell, Artistic Director, at hazell@unisono.net.mx.

Index